HEAVENLY
KNOWLEDGE

HEAVENLY KNOWLEDGE

AN ASTROPHYSICIST SEEKS WISDOM IN THE STARS

DR. FIORELLA TERENZI

AVON BOOKS NEW YORK

AVON BOOKS, INC.
1350 Avenue of the Americas
New York, New York 10019

Copyright © 1998 by Dr. Fiorella Terenzi
Front cover photograph of Dr. Terenzi by Lisa Peardon; photograph of sky by FPG
Interior design by Richard Oriolo
Published by arrangement with the author
ISBN: 0-380-79001-7
www.avonbooks.com

Library of Congress Cataloging in Publication Data:
Terenzi, Fiorella.
  Heavenly knowledge : an astrophysicist seeks wisdom in the stars / by Dr. Fiorella Terenzi.
    p. cm.
1. Astronomy—Popular works. 2. Astronomy—Philosophy—Popular works.
3. Astrophysics—Popular works. I. Title.
QB44.2.T47   1998   97-36745
520—dc21   CIP

First Avon Books Trade Paperback Printing: April 1999
First Avon Books Hardcover Printing: March 1998

AVON TRADEMARK REG. U.S. PAT. OFF. AND IN OTHER COUNTRIES, MARCA REGISTRADA, HECHO EN U.S.A.

Printed in the U.S.A.

OPM 10 9 8 7 6 5 4 3 2 1

It is to all women,

cast into silence and shadow

throughout these centuries of

scientific and astronomical discovery,

that I dedicate this book.

If I could, I would

repaint the celestial vault

with an equal number

of female and male

constellations.

HEAVENLY KNOWLEDGE

STELLAR HEART

I am five years old. I am walking hand in hand with my grandmother in the country outside of Milan. Our bare feet pad across the soft, damp grass. Alongside us, my little dog, Birba, scampers excitedly. Suddenly, my grandmother halts and points above us to the heavens.

Fiorella at Five Years Old

"Guarda! Look!" she says. "That star! The brightest one—she is looking at us!"

I laugh, but she goes on seriously. "Yes, piccola, all the stars have eyes to watch us. Look carefully!"

I do look carefully. And in that instant I feel the star gaze back at me. I feel as if it is a stellar heart that beats with mine. For a moment, all the loneliness of my childhood evaporates. I feel a peacefulness, a oneness with all of the Universe that I have never felt before.

"Remember this," my grandmother says. "Most people cannot look straight into a star's eyes. They are frightened and ashamed. But not you, Fiorella. You will always be able to feel the stars looking back at you."

Small Magellanic Cloud in the Southern Hemisphere
NATIONAL OPTICAL ASTRONOMY OBSERVATORIES

I often think about that first extraterrestrial gaze. How it made me quiver with awe. How it made me feel both like the center of the Universe and like an invisible microdot lost in incomprehensible space. I felt both magnificently empowered by this magical array of stellar jewelry and terribly humbled by the infinite vastness of it all. At that moment, I knew not a thing about quasars and black holes and brown dwarves; I did not even know that radio telescopes existed, let alone that at one point of my life I would spend years "peering" through one. All I knew was that the sky had suddenly opened up to me and I would never be the same again.

The first human must have felt something akin to this when she stepped out of her cave and turned her eyes skyward: shaken, empowered, humbled, mystified. What is this glorious display, this radiant cave ceiling that arches over the entire landscape? What is this fiery ball that cruises across the sky by day? This pale crescent that rises from behind the mountains and follows me through the night? And that sudden streak of light that leaves its ephemeral mark in the sky like a piece of stone scratched against the cave wall—what is that?

Am I a part of all of this? Can I ever know it? Does it know me? What does it tell me about my life? Can it show me how to construct my own internal universe?

For me, on the eve of the 21st Century with astounding new cosmic discoveries occurring at observatories almost daily, these first questions remain the most profound questions astrophysics can ask.

And yet somehow the sense of how I felt on that night with my grandmother easily fades from the professional astronomer's mind and heart, just as the sky fades from view when the lights of the cities emit an impenetrable pale curtain between earth and sky. We become

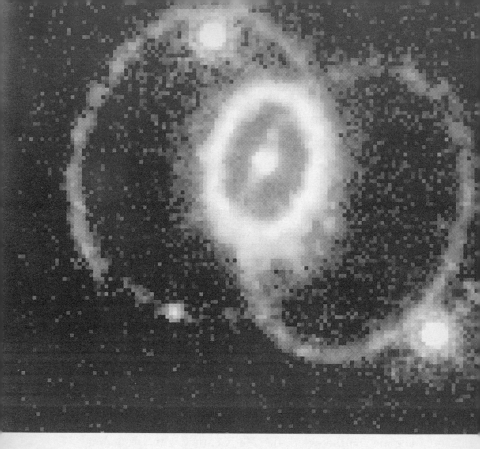

Supernova SN 1987A Double Ring
NASA

blinded by a technological barrier of abstract mathematical theorems and complex astronomical machinery, and we forget to feel the wonder of infinite space. We fail to communicate with loquacious celestial objects. We fall into the 20th Century trap of believing that the only knowledge we can gain from the Universe is objective facts and not poetic truths about our lives. We become

DR. FIORELLA TERENZI

4

deaf to the music of the spheres. And worst of all, we are afraid to look into the stars' eyes.

Heavenly Knowledge is my attempt to bring this sense of wonder back to astronomy. I enthusiastically embrace the fabulous new discoveries of astrophysics, but I do not want to stop there. I want these discoveries to swim in our imaginations, to open our hearts to new ways of thinking and feeling about life, about men and women, about catastrophes and rituals. I want us all to hear how the music of the spheres resonates with the music of our hearts.

THE UNIVERSE IS A BEAUTIFUL WOMAN

"We were goddesses before the sin
was put upon us."

Mars and Venus Cosmology

Strapped to my telescope atop Mount Palomar, I hit a switch
and the roof of the observatory grinds open, slowly revealing the

Cosmos. I type my password into the
computer and suddenly I feel myself
lift and spin like a child in a
carnival ride. I am rotating with the
stars—synchronized swimmers in the
heavens. I zero in on Stella Polaris,
the North Star, that fabulous
luminous circle, and once again I

Mount Palomar
FIORELLA TERENZI

find myself in the thrall of her exquisite beauty. Perfectly round,
elegant, so absolutely sure of her place in the heavenly order.
What a sexy enchantress!

Oh yes, the Universe is a beautiful woman.

*B*efore there was astronomy, there was cosmology—the philosophical study of the nature of the Universe. For the Greeks, this meant gazing into the sky and asking, What does all of this mean? How is the Universe structured? And above all, where does Humankind figure in this structure?

Even Plato, who was more inclined to stay indoors at night than to go out stargazing, wrote, "Had we never seen the stars, and the sun, and the heavens, none of the words which we have spoken about the universe would ever have been uttered. But now the sight of day and night, and the months and revolutions of the years, have created number, and have given us a conception of time, and the power of enquiring about the nature of the universe; and from this source we have derived philosophy, of which no greater good ever was or will be given by the gods to mortal man."

Not until centuries later, when science separated from philosophy to become a purely empirical enterprise that examined objects, measured them, charted their movements, and predicted their future behavior, did astronomy separate from purely human concerns. From then on, studying the stars had to be done dispassionately. After all, this was science—we dared not let our feelings and yearnings and personal quandaries become entangled in examining these celestial phenomena. We must be objective, the new scientists implored us. Our job is to master the Universe, not to commune with it.

Yet here I sit, my eye fixed to a giant, state-of-the-art telescope, convinced that we can do both—objectively learn about the Universe *and* commune with it. And as the 20th Century draws to a close, I believe it is high time we started some serious (and joyful) communing with the Universe.

I believe it takes a woman scientist to show us how to combine these seemingly opposite approaches to gazing at the stars. There is a growing campaign among my female colleagues in all of the sciences to give a human perspective to our work, to create a science that aspires to cooperate with Nature rather than to only quantify it. As the philosopher Mary Tiles says, we seek a science "which learns more by conversing . . . with Nature than by putting it on the rack to force it to reveal its secrets, a science of Venus rather than a science of Mars."

The proponents of the science of Mars are, of course, convinced that we Venus scientists are a bit soft in the head, that we have forsaken scientific objectivity in order to feel closer to our subject matter. But these Martians (as some of us are wont to call them) do not realize what we are up to. What we aim for is a *dynamic relationship* with data, a dance between the knower and the known. And if we indulge in metaphors for our lives drawn from what we ob-

Mars
JPL/NASA

Venus
JPL/NASA

serve, if we find lessons and poetry and music in what we see in the lenses of our microscopes and telescopes, we are not the less devoted to scientific truth. On the contrary, I am quite sure that we are more passionately in love with the truth than the "objective" observer who records his data without a flicker of emotion or even a momentary flight of imagination.

I remember when I was working on my doctorate in astrophysics at the University of Milan and one of my professors offered me what he considered a plum project for advancing my career: cataloging galaxies.

"Where would I do this cataloging?" I asked.

The professor indicated a windowless room in the basement filled with computers and file cabinets.

DR. FIORELLA TERENZI

"You mean, I wouldn't actually be looking at the stars?" I inquired.

The professor shrugged. Clearly he thought this was an irrelevant question.

"You'll get a fine paper out of it. Something eminently publishable," he responded, already showing some impatience with me.

But ambitious as I was, the idea of advancing my career in astronomy without actually gazing at the stars struck me as utterly preposterous. Sure, I would get my fill of data—declination and right ascension maps, logarithms of relative intensity and wavelength spectra—and I undoubtedly would be setting myself on the right track for a professorship, usually an impossible task for a woman scientist in Italy.

But without so much as a glimpse at the heavens? Without any opportunity for my nocturnal time-voyages to stars that had ceased to exist millions of years ago? No dancing with binary stars? No singing with Jupiter's moons?

I might just as well be sorting grades of pasta in that windowless basement room.

This was my introduction to the radical difference between the science of Mars and the science of Venus.

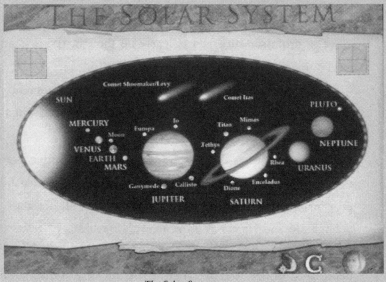

The Solar System
THE VOYAGER COMPANY, "INVISIBLE UNIVERSE" CD-ROM

THE SOLAR SYSTEM

About 10 billion years ago, the first stars formed in the disk of the Milky Way. One of these stars was our Sun and around it our planets. *Mercury*: one third the diameter of Earth and the closest of the nine planets to the Sun. *Venus*: similar to the Earth in size, mass, age and distance from the Sun but with temperatures that reach 475 degrees Centigrade. *Earth*: rich in life due to both an atmosphere that shields it from the Sun's deadly radiation and water which covers 71 percent of its surface. *Mars*: half the diameter of and 50 million miles farther from the Sun than Earth. *Jupiter*: largest planet in the solar system, 1900 times the mass of Earth and composed of nearly all gas. *Saturn*: almost ten times as far from the Sun as Earth, the second largest planet and famous for its rings. *Uranus*: −150 degrees Centigrade, rotates counterclockwise and ringed with icy black particles. *Neptune*: a near twin of Uranus in temperature and rotation, experiences a continual ferocious storm, equal in size to Earth's surface, called the Great Dark Spot. *Pluto*: the last and smallest planet, a cold ball of rock and ice with temperatures of −187 degrees Centigrade.

Worshiping the Goddess Through a Telescope

Through my work I want to bring back the sense of beauty and poetry to astronomy. I would like to help inspire a cosmology for the 21st Century based on the information and discoveries made available to us through modern technology—our satellites, radio telescopes, infrared imagers, and computers. I have no need to reinvent such a cosmology all by myself—I have lots of help. I can reach back long before the Greeks to a time when the Universe was seen as having a female shape, female sensibilities, and female sexuality—in short, a feminine Cosmic Order.

Before there were patriarchy and patriarchal religions, goddess worldviews and religions dominated the cultures of the world. These ancient goddesses embodied *all* the forces

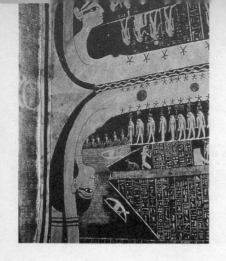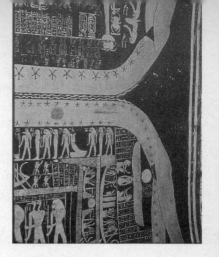

Nut, Egyptian Goddess of The Night Sky
E.C. KRUPP, GRIFFITH OBSERVATORY

of the Universe, both love *and* war, chastity *and* promiscuity, nurturing motherliness *and* bloodthirsty destructiveness. But above all, they presided over a universe that was constantly regenerating itself, a universe whose parts perished only to be reborn in a more evolved form.

This is precisely the universe that I see right now through my telescope, a universe where the supernova Tycho's Star explodes with such force that its heavy elements are scattered throughout the Cosmos, giving birth to new solar systems and planets like our own.

And everywhere I look, there are clusters of matter, of stars, of galaxies. Our own Milky Way circles close to the Andromeda Galaxy rather than occupying a piece of infinite

space all by itself. They call clusters and superclusters of gal-
axies "families," and rightly so. Gravitation is an organizing
principle, the pull of community, or interactivity, of
togetherness. It is so clear to me that gravity is a feminine
principle.

And now, as I direct the telescope over here, I see a dis-
tinctly feminine phenomenon, a globular cluster—perfectly
rounded and compressed at the center . . .

Whether they admit to it or not, the Mars scientists have unwittingly given us a cosmology, too, and it is light-years away from the cosmology of the goddesses. To begin with, these purely objective scientists have fostered a materialistic worldview—if there are only objects out there, and not subjects with which we can commune, we find ourselves isolated in a world of things. It is just Us (the observers) and Them (the things we observe), and our relationship to those things out there is reduced to possession, even if possessing celestial objects means no more than possessing knowledge about them.

Implicit in the Mars cosmology is the will to possession via domination. Mars is, after all, a god of war and war alone, not of war and rebirth. The final pillar of the Mars cosmology is religious nihilism. Don't be seduced by your spiritual yearnings, this worldview chides us, those are merely objects out there, random combinations of molecular material, nothing to get all awestruck and holy about.

Whirlpool Galaxy
NATIONAL OPTICAL ASTRONOMY OBSERVATORIES

WHIRLPOOL GALAXY

The spiral arms of this prototypical spiral galaxy make this galaxy look very much indeed like a whirlpool. In this visible light image, the gracefully sweeping arms are separated by lanes of interstellar gas and dust. Although they appear dark, these areas are actually filled with stars.

The most fascinating aspect of the Whirlpool system is that it is undergoing an interaction with another galaxy. Its companion can be seen at the top of this image. Because the space between stars is so great, such galaxy interactions will likely not result in the collision of even two stars. But the mutual gravitation of the two galaxies distorts them, twisting them into unusual shapes such as the bridge connecting the two of them.

Family of Stars: Globular Cluster NGC 5272
NATIONAL OPTICAL ASTRONOMY OBSERVATORIES

FAMILY OF STARS:
GLOBULAR STAR CLUSTER
NGC 5272

A dense, spherical group of mostly ancient stars, *globular clusters* surround the Milky Way and other galaxies. All of the stars in a globular cluster are thought to have formed at approximately the same time out of the same cloud of gas. These ancient star groups were shining long before our Sun was formed.

This globular cluster, NGC 5272, contains over 100,000 stars! It contains more known variable stars than any other cluster in the Milky Way. These stars, known as Cepheid Variables, become brighter and dimmer in a well understood pattern, making it possible to accurately determine their distance from us. NGC 5272 is 31,000 light-years away from Earth.

Not get awestruck? Not feel transcendentally transported when the Whirlpool Galaxy reels into view in the lens of my telescope, its graceful arms undulating like Shiva's in a glittering shower of stars and Cosmic dust?

I see (*and* hear) the Universe as a place of worship, the Original Cathedral after which the vaunted ceilings of Chartres, Canterbury, and Orvieto are all earthly imitations. I worship this goddess Universe through my telescope even as I chart galaxies and calculate their density and luminosity. I see myself as a part of this Universe I gaze into—an infinitely small but necessary part. Every celestial object I see through the giant telescope on Mount Palomar or through a radio telescope is a part of me and, as such, can inspire me as these stars and planets, comets and meteorites inspired architects and artists, musicians, poets and philosophers in earlier eras. And what is more, I can even become sensually entwined with these heavenly bodies.

Yes, it's true. Some would even say outrageously so . . .

My Celestial Lover

Orion swims into view in the lens of my telescope. Orion the Hunter—god, hero, warrior, son of Poseidon, tempestuous lover.

Suddenly, I am caught in his celestial light. It lures me

Orion Nebula
NATIONAL OPTICAL ASTRONOMY OBSERVATORIES

ORION NEBULA

This immense ocean of swirling, chaotic gas floating in space in the constellation Orion lives up to its name: *the Great Nebula in Orion*. The appearance of primeval turbulence is not mere fantasy. The nebula is, in fact, a huge stellar "nursery" in which thousands of young stars have been and are being formed out of enormous clouds of gas.

This large nebula shines because of the ultraviolet radiation of a cluster of hundreds of stars known as the Trapezium (as in *trapezoid*), which draws its name from its four brightest stars.

On a clear winter's night, you can actually see the brightest part of this great nebula without a telescope—the fuzzy central "star" in the sword of Orion is visible to the naked eye.

into Orion's Great Nebula, an immense, primeval ocean of swirling gases floating in space. I am drowning in it, gasping for air. I know that this nebula is a vast stellar nursery in which thousands of infant stars are constantly being born, fashioned from enormous clouds of ionized hydrogen and helium gases. It is visible to me only because of the ultraviolet radiation of a cluster of hundreds of bright young stars called the Trapezium. This stellar radiation is an ether that drugs me, makes my mind and heart soar.

Orion is looking back at me; I can feel it. His fiery explosions of passion make my body tremble. I gaze back at his constellation, a shining island lying just in front of a gigantic region of cold, dark, molecular hydrogen and helium. It is believed that new stars are forming here right now, although their newly emitted light is cloaked by the dark material from which they form and in which they are embedded. It is only a matter of time—mere millions of years—before the brightest of these stars will heat up new regions similar to Orion's Great Nebula.

But tonight, I feel the heat already.

Orion steps out of the rippled curtain of gas that marks the boundary between the hot gas of the Great Nebula and the cool, impenetrable molecular gas behind it. Burning sapphire emissions of sulfur atoms surround him. I watch breathlessly as the sulfur light forms clumps, filaments streaming from regions where the hot stars in the nebula are boiling off material of the molecular cloud.

Like a fountain spewing water, a young star in the Orion Nebula emits a jet of hot, compressed, ionized sulfur atoms into the surrounding gas and dust. I feel this jet passing through me. I shiver. I take a deep breath. Orion's jet stream is incredibly potent as it strikes the surrounding material, setting off a shock wave like an airplane crashing through the sound barrier.

I feel these shock waves surging through my body. If someone could look at me with infrared eyes, they would see my temperature rising on the stellar scale. Orion is burning, I am burning—we are enveloped in our own heat.

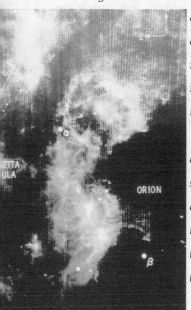

Orion Nebula in Infrared
JPL/IRAS

I see the hottest stars as blue-white dots. I sail past Betelgeuse, then Rigel, sail through luminous yellow hydrogen and oxygen clouds heated by clusters of hundreds of young, hot stars. I sweep through red-orange clouds of stars in the very process of forming.

I fly through it all into the arms of my hero, Orion. I feel his warmth *wrap around me. I feel hot like the newly formed stars in his nebula.*

Swirling around me are enormous purple and blue clouds of molecular carbon monoxide. I am floating on an ocean of molecules from which even now stars are taking shape as gas concentrations collapse under the force of gravity—not only hydrogen and carbon monoxide, but over thirty other different kinds of molecules. The mass of these clouds is stupefying—enough to make 700,000 stars the size of our Sun!

I feel contractions all over my body. I have a vision of other worlds being born, satellites to each one of these suns, exploding, multiplying. I feel Orion's touch. Out of his light, I feel life being created inside me. O Orion, my lover, my celestial lover.

And now I return to Earth, unstrap myself from the telescope, and step down onto the cold observatory floor. It is almost dawn. No one has arrived here yet, and I am relieved that I can still have a few moments alone. I check the computer to make sure all the data of my nocturnal adventure have been recorded properly, then turn it off and walk out into the sunlight, locking the door to the observatory behind me. Only then do I realize that I am soaked with sweat and I am trembling. . . .

Now, I ask you, Professore, is this any way for a Ph.D. astrophysicist to go about her work?

Absolutely!

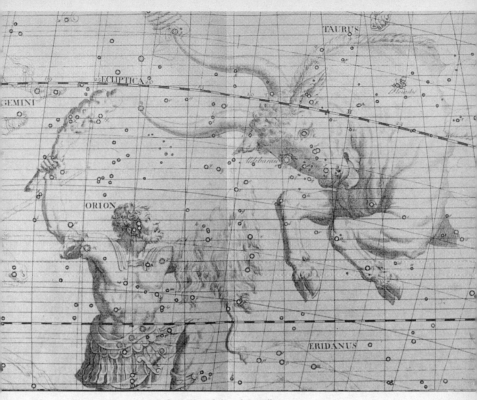

Orion As Mythological Constellation
OSSERVATORIO ASTRONOMICO, BRERA

A Cosmology for the 21st Century

I dream a cosmology for our time in which all the bodies
in the Universe are respected as teachers, inspirers, and,
yes, even as lovers.

I propose a cosmology for our time in which everything
that exists is viewed as having a life of its own in the broad-
est ontological sense of the word.

I dream a cosmology in which reason and imagination are not enemies, but rather partners in appreciation of the wonders of the Universe.

I propose a cosmology in which the accidents of Nature are probed for meanings as well as for functions and in which chaos is seen as mysterious rather than as irrational.

I dream a cosmology in which women and men on Planet Earth are a part of the Universal Picture, not the center of it—and certainly not the owners of it.

I propose a cosmology for our time in which Beauty is worshiped in whatever form it takes—a leaf, a song, a shooting star.

I dream a cosmology where the constellations of the night sky have female and male names in equal number.

I dream a cosmology in which the Universe is a beautiful woman.

Female Constellation: Cassiopeia

OSSERVATORIO ASTRONOMICO, BRERA

Female Constellation: Virgo

OSSERVATORIO ASTRONOMICO, BRERA

Male Constellation: Bootes

OSSERVATORIO ASTRONOMICO, BRERA

Male Constellation: Hercules

OSSERVATORIO ASTRONOMICO, BRERA

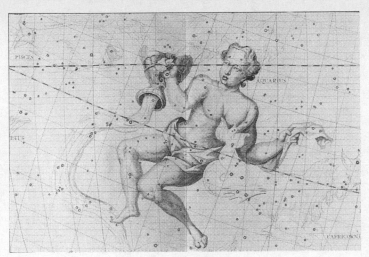

Male Constellation: Aquarius
OSSERVATORIO ASTRONOMICO, BRERA

Male Constellation: Cepheus
OSSERVATORIO ASTRONOMICO, BRERA

I HEAR THE
UNIVERSE SINGING

"In the Beginning was the Vibration,
And the Vibration resonated, building to a Crescendo,
And from that Crescendo came the Eternal Song of the Expanding
Universe"

Bursting with Song

The most ecstatic moments of my life have been when I burst out with song, when a tiny vibration within me built with a passion so intense that I could no longer contain it.

I first became aware of this when I was a child of perhaps six or seven out on one of my night prowls with my grandmother. There was a particularly bright sky, a full moon, Venus vividly ascending, the Big Dipper so well defined that I felt I could reach up and trace its outline with my fingertip. Gazing heavenward, I began to feel the most peculiar sensation somewhere deep inside my chest. It was at once calming and distressing, a feeling of profound serenity assailed

My Grandmother Angela
FIORELLA TERENZI

by a feeling of desperate longing. I knew even then that this serenity was born of my feeling of oneness with the Universe. But the *longing*—what was that?

At that moment, I heard a dog somewhere on the hillside start to howl. And suddenly I knew exactly what my feeling of longing was all about: I wanted to *connect* with everything out there. I wanted to shout, "Look at me! I am a part of this glorious Cosmos!" I wanted to participate in the noise of the Universe. *I wanted to join in the Cosmic Song!*

That is when it burst out of me—part swoon, part primordial wail, part lyrical incantation. Without thinking about it, without even knowing that it was going to happen, I began to sing a song without words to the sky above me.

I was barely conscious of my grandmother standing beside me as my song went on and on, now soaring, now a pulsing sound coming straight from my heart. When I had finally finished, she took my hand and squeezed it. My grandmother knew this song.

Over the years, other songs have burst out of me—songs of love, songs of loss, songs of exhilaration, songs of total happiness. But they do not come so easily now. Self-consciousness gets between me and my spontaneous song. I too easily become trapped by words without a melody. I wish I had a recording of that first song I sang to the sky on that country hillside. It was the most heartfelt song that ever burst out of me.

On that night I did not, of course, have the faintest idea what the Big Bang theory was. But years later, when I learned about such phenomena at the university, I found myself smiling.

Of course, I thought. *I know that song. It is the First Song and it is the Last Song.*

A Big Bang Fantasy

As a Milanese teenager, I would go out dancing with my friends almost every Friday and Saturday night, and we would lose ourselves to the disco beat. Today dancing is still one of my favorite pastimes, whether I am in New York or Los Angeles, whether the music is techno or ambient. What I am always fascinated by when I go to a club is the spinning mirrored ball on the ceiling above the center of the dance floor.

As I dance directly under the mirrored ball, I watch the reflected dots of white light playing on the walls and floor, always spinning, always reaching outward. The music throbs, and I feel as if I am at the center of an expanding universe of orbiting celestial bodies, a universe of light spinning around me. The farther from their source the light spots are thrown, the farther apart they become, like galaxies eternally chasing an ever-expanding space. In modern astrophysics theory, that source, the Beginning of All Matter and Time, is known by the explosive name of the Big Bang.

In every time and in every culture, cosmology has sought an account of the Beginning, a First Cause for the Universe and everything within it. This is the starting point from which all cultural knowledge follows: It explains what there is and how it got here. All the rest—*why* it is here and *what* is good or bad about it—is the culture's philosophy.

In ancient cosmologies and primitive myths, the First Cause ranges from a volcanic burst to the cracking open of an enormous egg, but what a great many of these stories have in common is that the beginning of all time and matter was *an explosive acoustical event*. These myths propose that it all started with a thunderclap, a primordial explosion, a shout. The Saravastian (Hindu) story begins with

THE BIG BANG

The Big Bang, the moment of genesis for our entire Universe, was much more than an explosion that spewed forth all the matter and energy that fills the Cosmos. It was the event that created both space and time! In a sense, the Big Bang happened everywhere at once, and after that moment of creation, space itself began stretching and expanding at a phenomenal rate. As space expands, the contents of space, energy and hot gases, spread out and cool off in the process. Indeed, in the first moments of the Universe, even the basic laws of physics we know today were different, simpler.

Eventually the temperature lowered enough to produce familiar particles of matter such as protons and electrons, which, after about 700,000 years, cooled enough to pair off and form atoms of hydrogen gas. The influence of gravity, acting on a residual clumpiness left over from the earliest instants of time, soon drew together vast clouds of gas that would continue to collapse to form clusters of galaxies, galaxies, stars, and planets. But space continues to expand, with all parts of the Universe rushing away from all other parts. The galaxies, like beads on an ever-stretching string, continue to grow more distant from one another.

the ripples of a shapeless creature that gradually transform themselves into a soft, whispery sound, which in turn billows to a single syllable that echoes throughout the void: "Ommmmmmmm." And, of course, the Bible states, "In the beginning was the word"—the spirit of God formed into sound.

Modern astrophysical theory for the origin of the Universe is also expressed as an explosive event: the Big Bang. To be sure, the Big Bang theory cannot be categorized as simply another myth; it is a scientific theory with a whole array of testable hypotheses about the age, shape, and size of the Universe. Yet for the majority of the human population who have not grasped the abstract subtleties of the Big Bang theory (and may not be entirely sure that they even want to try), the Big Bang has mythological impact.

The Big Bang is what most people are alluding to when they say that they believe in a *scientific* explanation for the origin of the Universe as compared with biblical Creationism. But the Big Bang also provides us with a simple mental construct with which to ponder the almost-unimaginable idea of a beginning for time and space. It gives us an artful model that we can try to wrap our minds around: a thundering explosion of cosmic proportions that still echoes in the Universe much as the Hindus speculated about a primordial sound that still hums out there.

DR. FIORELLA TERENZI

MICROWAVE BACKGROUND RADIATION

Radiation left over from when the Universe was less than a million years old can now be detected as microwaves coming from all directions in the sky. This "afterglow" is considered evidence of the Big Bang.

But we are still stuck with the question: What caused this *first* explosion?

Although there is now substantial agreement in the scientific community about what happened *after* the Big Bang, only a few physicists attempt to address the question of what happened "before the beginning." We try to compute a model that simulates the Big Bang in order to come up with a hypothesis for this First Cause, but a definitive answer eludes us. What in the world can it mean to say that before the Big Bang neither time nor space existed? When was this "then" that antedated time? Whenever I try to think about the mind-boggling concept of a First Cause, I am reminded of an exchange attributed to the pre-Socratic philosopher Heracleitus and a student of his. Heracleitus had just taught the boy that the god Atlas carries the world on his shoulders.

"But what does Atlas stand on?" the student asked.

"He stands on the back of a turtle," the philosopher replied.

"Yes, but what does the turtle stand on?" the student pressed on.

"It stands on the back of another turtle," Heracleitus answered.

"And that turtle—what does *he* stand on?" the student shot back triumphantly.

Heracleitus shook his head patiently.

"It's turtles all the way down!" he explained.

As for me, I like to fantasize that there are *vibrations* all the way down. I think of the resonance effect when an acute, high-pitched sound shatters a long-stemmed glass— *Bang!* I think of a thunderstorm gathering in the sky, the electric energy building until it explodes—*Bang!* I think of all the other, relatively smaller, cosmic explosions—such as the exploding stars that created our planets and, ultimately, the life that exists on our Earth. I think of the human reproductive explosions that continually replicate that life. *Exploding energy echoing everywhere.*

In this scenario, I like to imagine that the Big Bang was the result of the tiniest of quivers, a resonance effect that built over an eternity of pre-time until it had to escape— then the explosion, an expansion of space through time, an expansion with no center that was happening everywhere at once. All matter spread itself out in lower densities as it followed the expansion of space.

It is only a fantasy, this First Quiver, this acoustical debut, this sound that lingers in the Universe—it is definitely *not* a scientific theory. I still eagerly await a straightforward and definitive explanation for the First Cause from my colleagues in physics and mathematics, yet at this moment in astronomic history it remains one of the Great Unknowns. So for now, my fantasy First Quiver is a myth our earthly minds can play with.

Hearing and Seeing— Sense and Sensibility

Since ancient times, humankind has investigated life and the Universe *visually*—designing graphs and visual models to represent every phenomenon encountered. If there was a mystery out there, it was captured in an image, a visual representation. In the modern era, this meant taking *invisible* entities—such as celestial objects that cannot be perceived by even our most powerful optical telescopes—and rendering them as some kind of picture or radio map. Data received via a radio telescope is "translated" into radio maps and diagrams.

Early on in my education, I began to wonder about

ELECTROMAGNETIC
SPECTRUM

Our world is continually bathed in light from the Sun, the Moon, the planets, and the stars. However, the light we see—visible light—represents just a small portion of a much larger picture: a continuum of energy known as the Electromagnetic Spectrum.

Since our atmosphere prevents many kinds of electromagnetic radiation from reaching us, Earthbound telescopes can view only visible light and radio waves. Observations of other wavelengths require satellites placed above Earth's atmosphere.

The behavior of electromagnetic radiation depends on its wavelength. Radiation with very long wavelengths can easily penetrate certain substances but carries very little energy. Radiation with shorter wavelengths is more powerful and is more likely to affect the structure of the material it encounters.

Radio waves are at the longest end of the spectrum, with wavelengths ranging from centimeters to kilometers. Their large size makes them ideal for television and radio broadcasts—they can go through solid structures more easily than other types of radiation. In space, radio waves are often generated by energetic electrons traveling through ionized gas.

Microwave radiation has shorter wavelengths of only several millimeters. Best known for its use in heating food, it is also used for communications. Celestial microwave emissions often come from dense, cool interstellar clouds.

We cannot see infrared light, but we can feel it as heat on our skin. Emitted by many objects in space, such as grains of interstellar dust and cool giant stars, infrared light occupies the wavelength region around a millionth of a meter.

Visible light, emitted by most stars, occupies a very, very narrow region compared with the full range of electromagnetic radiation. Convention has broken visible light down into seven colors, each color corresponding to a slightly different wavelength: red, orange, yellow, green, blue, indigo, and violet.

Often generated by very hot gases, ultraviolet light is invisible to our eyes. However, it has a visible effect on our skin—tanning and burning.

With wavelengths less than a billionth of a meter, X rays can pass right through certain materials, such as the human body. But their high energy means they can also be agents of destruction to living tissue.

Gamma rays have the highest energy of any type of electromagnetic radiation, and along with X rays are associated with the most spectacularly powerful events in the universe, such as superheated gases falling into black holes and neutron stars. With wavelengths ranging from a trillionth of a meter to a thousandth of a trillionth of a meter, gamma rays are roughly the size of the nucleus of an atom.

other possibilities for representing the world and the Universe besides a visual correlative. Although we first became aware of celestial objects by gazing up at the night sky, we now know that what we can actually *see*—even with the aid of an optical telescope—comprises a tiny fraction of what is technologically detectable out there.

So why is it that when we receive emissions from the Universe we immediately attempt to make *visual* sense out of them, that we reflexively create graphs and curves and diagrams? We receive vibrations from the Cosmos and our first instinct is to draw a map. Why do we confine ourselves to this one sensibility?

This question sang loudly in my mind during the period of my life when I was studying astrophysics at the University of Milan by day and studying opera and musical theory in the *Corsi Popolari* at the Giuseppe Verdi Conservatorio by night. I would go from calculating the luminosity and magnitude of celestial bodies in a classroom on one side of the city to singing scales and arpeggios in a classroom on the other side of the city with just a quick slice of pizza and a Metropolitana ride in between.

I am living in two universes and they are worlds apart. . . .

Here at the university, my left brain is a focused beam of white light, clean, precise, digital. I concentrate, I reason, I solve. I feel exhilarated by the power of the analytic mind.

DR. FIORELLA TERENZI

Yet throughout the day I feel a strange pressure building inside me—creative energy yearning to explode.

And now at the Conservatorio, my right brain takes over. I am overwhelmed with emotion—the suffering and tears of the operatic heroines. Emotion that cannot be analyzed and digitalized. Finally, that vibrating emotion must crack through. Only music will do. I explode in song.

Shuttling back and forth between these two universes, I start asking myself fundamental questions: What gives us more complete information, sound or images? How does acoustic memory compare with visual memory?

Today, I am sitting in the giardini pubblici with people talking all around me. I can hear sounds coming at me from every direction, but I can see only in the direction I point my eyes. Does this mean I am more immersed in the sounds around me than in the images around me? Am I more at the center of my acoustical world than my visual world? I jot these questions down in the notebook I carry with me everywhere.

A truck passes by. I can hear it on the road behind me. I know it is a truck by its sound, without having to look. I note this observation, too.

It is later in the afternoon. I have been studying for hours. I put down my books and close my eyes, exhausted by reading. But suddenly a thought occurs and my notebook is out again. "Eyes tire, ears don't," I write.

Now it is night. I am abruptly awakened from a deep sleep by the racket of a motor scooter revving under my bedroom window. Again, I reached for my notebook: "Ears don't sleep—eyes do. Eyes need light—ears don't."

Yes, these are obvious observations. But I keep thinking that they all add up to something significant about the differences between the way we process aural information and the way we process visual information.

I realize one big difference is in how we remember this information. A song can ignite a detailed memory of a whole period of my life much more effectively than anything visual—including a photograph—can. Just a hint of melody can summon up a particular romance, a kiss when that song played in the background, a car trip as a child when a certain piece of music played on the radio. Aural memories feel much more intimate to me.

I also realize that my visual mind has much less tolerance for redundancy than my aural mind does. I can watch the same movie only a few times before feeling I've had quite enough—but I can listen to the same piece of music over and over endlessly without tiring of it.

I am sitting in the subway, the *Metropolitana,* looking over what I have written in my notebook. Now there is not a doubt in my mind: Auditory information has something important to offer us that visual information does not.

DR. FIORELLA TERENZI

*But what does all of this mean about the celestial objects
I am studying?*

Cosmic Waves/Musical Notes

It is late June in Milan. The five of us studying astrophysics
and radio astronomy are the only ones left at the university—every other student is on vacation. The word *radio*
seems to occur half a dozen times in every sentence the
professor utters: "*Radio* waves coming from *radio* galaxies
are decoded for intensity and frequency like *radio* waves
from other *radio* objects, whether or not they are in the
radio sky." The blackboard is strewn with radio frequencies:
"1420 megahertz—hydrogen," "110 gigahertz—methyl
alcohol molecule."

Then, as always, I race off to the Corsi Popolari di
Musica at the Conservatorio and slide into my seat at the
back of the lecture hall. Here, the blackboard is covered
with tonalities: "A major," "D minor."

"Frequency represents cycles per second, how many
times the vibration goes back and forth in a single second,
and this is measured in Hertz," the professor is saying.
"Thus, one cycle per second equals one Hertz, one hundred
cycles per second equals one hundred Hertz, and so on."

Sure, I think, gazing out the window into the summer

night. *I've heard this all before—Hertz and megahertz and gigahertz and terahertz.*

"A loud sound has greater intensity than a soft sound," the professor goes on.

Yes, yes, I think. *Just like the varying intensities of the radiation waves striking the Earth.*

"The A to which we tune the orchestra's instruments vibrates at 440 cycles per second—what we call 440 Hertz," the music professor continues. "And the human voice—our own natural instrument—has a range of vibrations from 27 to 4,186 Hertz."

I wonder about the incredibly high pitch of the "voices" of the galaxies—1 billion to 1,000 billion Hertz! This is way beyond our human auditory range, which is between 20 and 20,000 Hertz.

But wait a moment—Why am I even thinking about the "voices" out there in the Cosmos?

In that instant I realized what all my questions about sight and sound had been leading up to. . . .

I long to hear the stars! I want to be sensually immersed in the Universe. I want to feel the Cosmos coming at me from every direction. I want it to excite my emotions through the same sense that music does. And I want it to stay in my auditory memory in the same way, too. Yes, yes, I yearn to hear the stars!

*And the key is within my reach—intensity and fre-
quency! They decode* both *radio waves from space* and *musical tones. They will help me render heavenly bodies into
auditory "shapes."*

*I can hear it now—a Universe of sound parallel to the
visible Universe! An acoustic Universe!*

The very next morning in my radio astronomy course,
I hung on every word the professor uttered. I had been the
first to arrive in class and now I was the first to raise my
hand with a question.

"What would we see if we could perceive the radio sky
with our eyes?" I asked.

A bit taken aback, the professor replied that if we could
see radio waves instead of light, the sky would look entirely
different.

"Daytime would be as dark as night," he said. "The
stars would be invisible. The Milky Way and celestial objects would look like huge nebulae, strange-shaped clouds
of hot interstellar gases, a high-energy filament spread out
across the sky."

Interesting, I thought.

"*Professore,* what if we could *hear* the radio sky?"

The professor hesitated before answering my question.

"We cannot listen to cosmic radio waves the way you

Radio Galaxy: Centaurus A
NATIONAL OPTICAL ASTRONOMY OBSERVATORIES

RADIO GALAXY:
CENTAURUS A

A radio galaxy is one that produces a large amount of energy in the form of radio waves. This emission often comes from large structures that appear to be two more or less symmetric lobes around the center of the galaxy. The famous radio galaxy *Centaurus A* is the closest high-energy galaxy to us, with an active nucleus that emits tremendous amounts of radio and X-ray radiation.

The nuclear activity may be fueled by gas that falls into a massive black hole in Centaurus A's center. One of the most interesting aspects of this galaxy is the unusual black belt that stretches across the galaxy's middle. An obscuring layer made up of clouds of gas and dust, this "dust lane" sucks up much of the galaxy's light; but Centaurus A is so amazingly bright that it is still one of the brightest galaxies in the Virgo supercluster.

listen to your radio at home," he began. "We convert those emissions into images—more like a television picture—with the help of a radio telescope. Radio waves from celestial objects are not pure; they are out of sync with one another. Convert them to sound and all you will hear is static."

"Are you saying there is no way we can listen to what is out there?" I asked.

"It's a totally different phenomenon," the professor replied impatiently. "In any event, there have been no experiments to see if sound has any use in astronomy, among other reasons because there are no tools for doing so. *Sound has no place in astronomy.*"

Doesn't it? Now I was even more curious about an audible Universe. I still wanted to know if sound could provide us with some kind of information that might be hidden in a visual representation of celestial radiations. Wasn't there *some* way I could transform galactic radio waves into sounds that humans could hear?

How? Where were the tools I needed?

Acoustic Astronomy—the Song of Songs

The American Library of Milan lies in the elegant historic center of the city among stately palazzos and trendy shops.

But everywhere I look are polizia guarding this grand American palace of information from terrorist attacks.

Usually, I come here to check up on NASA's latest discoveries, but today I am on quite a different mission.

Fiorella at UCSD
D. REISNER

My colleagues at the University of Milan have informed me that the most up-to-date work in computer-generated sound is being done at university laboratories in the United States—and not simply in computer-generated sound, but in computer-generated music. As I leaf through American university catalogs, in my mind's ear I hear the eerie, strangely stirring strains of a Ligeti composition, the first computer music I ever heard. This music was produced via computer analysis, synthesis, and processing, and that is exactly what I am searching for—some kind of sound synthesis software to use to convert galactic waves into audible sound.

Already, I am playing with ideas for names for this new technique of listening to the galaxies. Shall I call it Radio Computer Music Astronomy? How about simply Acoustic Astronomy? Yes, that's it—Acoustic Astronomy!

In the catalogs, I narrow down my options to MIT's Experimental Music Studio, Stanford's Center for Computer Research in Music and Acoustics, and the University of California at San Diego's Center for Music Experiment.

I write to UCSD, explaining why I want to do the work for my doctoral thesis in astronomy at its Center for Music Experiment. UCSD replies immediately: Yes, they are more than interested in my project—they are excited by it!

Suddenly, I was in California. If I had any doubt that the plane had landed in the right place, all I had to do was look around me: Instead of the familiar panorama of churches and statues, gates and monuments, I saw 360 degrees of palm trees, sun, ocean, and beach. Yes, I was in California!

At the Center for Music Experiment, I focused first on how to create sounds via computer, then on a galaxy hidden from our eyes in the direction of Coma Berenices, deep in the darkness between Virgo and Leo, under the handle of the Big Dipper. Galaxies we cannot see rarely earn beautiful names, and this one was no exception: It was known as Radio Galaxy UGC 6697. When I began my experiment, astrophysicists had already used huge radio telescopes to collect radiation that had traveled 180 million light-years from UGC 6697. These scientists had converted the galaxy's

U G C   6 6 9 7

UGC 6697 is an unusual radio source whose associated galaxy, Zwicky 97087 (and several companion galaxies), seems to be plowing through the Coma supercluster to the supercluster's center, with gas and dust being stripped in the process and streaming out behind it. This very energetic object emits radiation at almost all wavelengths, including X-ray wavelengths. It is also the site of very active star formation.

A radio galaxy's characteristic pair of huge diffuse lobes indicate its central, compact, solar-system-size radio source, from which radio waves pour forth. This source connects to the lobes via jets that spit out material that travels at close to the speed of light. The Coma Berenices supercluster is comprised of thousands of galaxies densely packed at its core.

radiations into radio photographs—*images*. I was going to use the same data to create *sounds*—to start to decode the sonorous Universe.

Using some remarkable new sound synthesis software called "cmusic," I began the laborious process of converting the radiation's frequency and intensity into an audible signal—into *acoustic vibrations*.

It is a labor of love and infinite patience. . . .
I am using data from the Very Large Array radio tele-

D R .   F I O R E L L A   T E R E N Z I

scope in Socorro, New Mexico, with its twenty-seven disklike antennae pointing at the same celestial object. At its peak, this radio telescope generates about 10 million numbers per minute that are stored in a computer—an impressive number, especially when you realize that a single radio image can require up to forty hours of observation!

Months of study go by—research, coding, testing, debugging—the long prelude to the big moment.

It is early morning at the laboratory in San Diego. I immediately go to the computer to check its progress.

"Working," the computer flashes back at me. "Working."

I sigh. It has been like this for weeks. Sharing the huge computer with other researchers has slowed me down. Every day I have to make adjustments, negotiate, and find spaces on the computer where I can store masses of data. How long can it take?

Another morning, the same message—"Working . . . Working."

"Wonderful," I say to the computer under my breath. "You are working, but I am waiting!"

Weeks go by. "Working . . . Working . . ." I am beginning to wonder if the program is processing the data properly. Have I got it right? Has all of my work been in vain? Is it impossible after all, this crazy idea of hearing a galaxy 180 million light-years away? Am I wasting my time on a fantasy?

Very Large Array Radio Telescope, Socorro, New Mexico
MICHAEL GASTALDO

VERY LARGE ARRAY
RADIO TELESCOPE

Located in New Mexico, the *Very Large Array radio telescope* (VLA) is made up of twenty-seven radio dishes mounted in a Y-shaped formation. Radio waves are collected by the individual dishes and are transported to a control building, where computers process the data to create a radio picture.

Each radio dish is mounted on a rail car so that it can be moved from time to time a range of over twenty miles to achieve different resolutions. Although each dish is eighty-two feet in diameter, the surface of each is constructed with an accuracy of 0.05 inch.

Another week passes. "Working," the computer flashes back at me. . . .

This morning I have to drag myself out of bed to go to the laboratory. This daily trip has become like a visit to a lover who has lost all interest in me, who is too preoccupied to even say hello. Mechanically, I type my password into the computer, a rote exercise in futility. But suddenly a new word is flashing back at me: "Ready."

I cannot believe it. Did I type in the wrong password? Am I dreaming this moment that I have rehearsed in my mind a thousand times?

"Ready," the computer flashes back at me.

My God, all I have to do is press "Play" and I will hear the sounds I have gathered from the other side of the Universe!

I hesitate. I do not want to be alone for this moment. I go to the telephone and start calling friends and colleagues in the department. Within a few minutes they are all here, packed into this tiny room at the laboratory, looking at me, silently waiting.

The computer is ready and I am ready, too. I press the key, "Play." For what seems like an eternity, nothing issues from the speakers.

And then it begins, the Galactic Symphony. The sounds that fill that little room are haunting, ethereal, powerful, and violent, and at the same time so literally otherworldly that we

*are all struck dumb—staring, listening. It is unlike anything
I have ever heard before: Cosmic pulsing, high-pitched overtones mixed with static. It is coming in nonhuman frequencies
that resonate at the base of my spine and then reverberate up
my nervous system to my brain, shaking me loose of my terrestrial moorings.*

*These sounds are coming across 180 million light-years of
space, which means that they are coming across 180 million
years of time. This wondrous symphony is being broadcast
from what had been the Jurassic Age on Earth, eons before
the first human stood upright.*

*My heart almost explodes! I can barely catch my breath.
I am listening to an echo of the Original Galactic Song! I
am listening to the galaxy UGC 6697 as it existed in
prehistory.*

*The sounds end. Everyone remains silent for several sec-
onds and then suddenly they are all cheering, shouting. It
goes on for several minutes and then, one by one, my friends
and colleagues approach me, shake my hand, embrace me, kiss
me, and then, one by one, file out.*

For the days and weeks that followed, I walked around
with those sounds reverberating in my mind. Hearing the
sounds of UGC 6697 across the millennia was probably as
close to a life-changing experience as I had ever had in my
adult life. I felt awed and strangely helpless. During that

time, there was no way I could force myself to go directly back to the business of writing up my results, completing my dissertation, submitting it to my professors and to professional journals. That all seemed so banal, so trivial compared to what I was feeling. But time was tight, and I had to put my results into an academic context I could present back at the University of Milan.

I returned home to Milan. My dissertation defense date was set promptly. And when the fateful day arrived, a long table of fifteen professors was waiting for me.

I mounted the platform, placed all my transparencies in the projector, and immediately began to describe my work on representing celestial radiation through sound.

"Acoustic Astronomy is an alternative we can use in addition to visual and other techniques," I told them. "It is based on an analogy between radiation and musical notes. What I was seeking was a kind of sonic signature for each celestial object."

I quickly glanced up and surveyed their faces. They were all eyes, all ears. I was afraid to look back at them too closely for fear of losing my concentration while trying to read their expressions. I went on. And then the inevitable question came.

"Excuse me, *signorina*," a professor began. "But what could a sound representation possibly reveal that a visual representation could not?"

My reply was ready and well-rehearsed. I exploded with all the hypotheses I had been working on. First, I emphasized the idea that sound in astronomy might reveal information that is not easily observed with a visual representation. From there, I went on to discuss acoustic phenomena—like the Doppler effect—that we are familiar with in everyday life but that also could apply to celestial objects we might "listen to." And from there I went to binary star systems where radiations with almost identical frequencies could generate beats—yes, the same kind of beats we use when we tune a musical instrument.

I journeyed on with a description of further tests and experiments that could be done to develop and test my technique: with quasars, with the compression and decompression of the solar core, with pulsar pulses—what I called "cosmic drummers."

I was so caught up in my detailed reply that it was only when I had finished and looked up that I saw that all the professors were totally captivated by my theories—at least that's what I desperately hoped their rapt expressions meant. There was a long moment of silence while we all caught our breath. And then the president of the commission thanked me for my presentation and asked me to please wait outside while they discussed my work. I left the room, my heart beating frantically.

What followed was perhaps the longest three hours of

my life. In the course of that time, I convinced myself that the reason they were taking so long was because they were trying to figure out a way to turn me down politely. Finally, they called me back in to hear their decision.

"Congratulations, *Dottore Terenzi*," the president said.

Dottore Fiorella Terenzi! After years of study I had been granted my doctorate in physics with a specialization in astrophysics.

My life literally changed overnight. The next morning I was awakened by a call from a Milanese newspaper. They had heard about this new world of Acoustic Astronomy and they wanted to interview me. In a matter of weeks, I was a guest on every radio and television talk show in Italy and on the BBC. On top of everything else, I was offered a job teaching at the Liceo Scientifico Marangoni, at which I had once been a student.

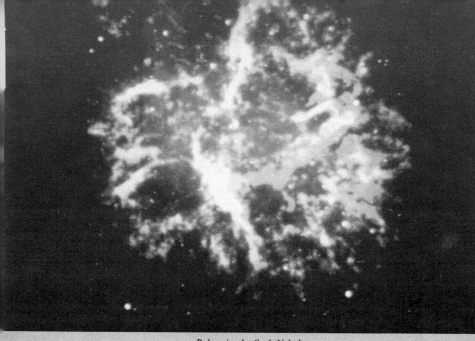

Pulsar in the Crab Nebula
NATIONAL OPTICAL ASTRONOMY OBSERVATORIES

PULSAR IN THE
CRAB NEBULA

With its clawlike streamers of gas, the *Crab Nebula* in the constellation Taurus is "living" evidence of one of the most spectacular astronomical events: a supernova explosion. Known as a supernova remnant, it is the debris of the explosion of a massive star.

Near the center of this photograph lies a faint object, the Crab Pulsar, whose pulses come at intervals of .033 second, which means that the object is rotating more than thirty times per second—a very fast "cosmic drummer."

In fact, its spectacular birth was observed by the astronomers of the Imperial Court of the Sung Dynasty in

China in 1054. According to the Chinese astronomers, the "guest star" could be seen in broad daylight for three weeks, was bright in the night sky for six months, and then finally disappeared. Although there are no existing contemporaneous European records of the event, Native American pictographs made at around the same time in northern Arizona depict a crescent moon and a bright star in approximately the same relative locations as the Moon and supernova would have been on the day the explosion was first visible on Earth.

Three

DIVADOC

"When learning finds an emotional home,
what is learned is learned forever."

From Astrophysicist to
Recording Artist

*T*eaching turned out to be wonderfully gratifying. I
loved my students, all of them, and they appeared to
enjoy my classes very much. One day the *Preside* (headmistress) of the school approached me in the corridor to tell
me how amazed she was that my students were always smiling.

"On the way to gym I might expect such smiles," she
told me. "But on their way to math and physics? That's a
first for this school. How do you account for it?"

I told her that I always tried to make my lessons relevant
to their real lives. A student comes in wearing a pop star
T-shirt and suddenly we are talking about how the image
was printed on the cloth—an entire discussion of the concept of "pressure" follows. A math problem begins with a
discussion of breakfast cereals; the notions of time and mo-

tion are illustrated by popular music videos. I was convinced that there was not a concept in all of physics that I could not put in the context of their young lives—and my idea was working. It was a technique that would continue to serve me well when I appeared on the stage.

Yet, happy and gratified as I was in the classroom, something deep inside kept tugging at me. *It was that song. . . .*

On that extraordinary day in San Diego when I had pressed "Play" and first heard the Galactic Symphony, I had immediately transferred the Cosmic sounds to a simple cassette. And when I was back in Milan, I played it over and over again in my apartment. It always had the same effect on me. . . .

My Students at Liceo Scientifico

I am dizzy. These sounds pull me out of my skin for a weightless journey through time and space. And I feel as if I will never come back.

My classes today are over earlier than usual. I return to my apartment and make myself a sandwich. I take it to my bed, then place the cassette in my player and turn it on. As I listen carefully, these galactic sounds again transport me. But this time just listening is not enough. Something is missing— some personal connection. I look up and see my keyboard standing next to my desk. I switch it on. Yes, this is what I have wanted to do from that instant when I first heard these sounds. I want to jam with the Universe! I want to be a part of that celestial music. A song bursts out of me.

If ever the music I have composed was purely inspired, this is it. If ever improvisation poured out of me without a thought, without a trace of self-consciousness intervening, this is it. I feel as if I am in the thrall of some power that comes from beyond anything I can see or touch.

I play along with the sounds of UGC 6697 for two or three hours, pausing only to restart the cassette. Thankfully, I realize that what is happening is extraordinary and quite possibly unrepeatable, so I record every note I play. It is as if I already know that this tape will contain the seeds of almost a dozen musical compositions and songs that I will develop and play in concerts in the years to come.

After that fateful afternoon, I began experimenting with this cosmic music in a professional recording studio.

Somebody Out There Is Listening

One afternoon, my duties at the school ran late and I had to race to the studio for my scheduled time—every minute there is extremely costly. I was once again sitting in Studio B of a major recording facility in Milan, downloading my radio astronomical sounds to the computer hard disk for further filtering and cleaning up. There was a sharp knock at my door. I paused and walked to the door and open it.

A youngish man with a vaguely familiar face smiled at me.

"Hi, I'm Rob Fraboni. I'm mixing a record for Robert Palmer in Studio A, and every time I take a break, I hear these extraordinary sounds coming from in here. In my business, you hear all kinds of stuff all the time, but this is unlike anything I've ever heard. What on earth are you doing in here?"

I told him I was downloading galactic sounds from 180 million light-years away, then explained a bit about my experiments in Acoustic Astronomy.

"What?" he said. "Mind if I take a listen close up?"

"Sure." I offered him a seat and switched on the Galactic Symphony. His reaction was now familiar to me—that faraway look of being transported in time and space. After several minutes, he signaled for me to stop the tape and asked if he could use my phone. He dialed a long-distance number.

"Chris? You won't believe this! I'm here in the recording studio with an Italian astrophysicist. She just played for me sounds that are literally from outer space. It's dynamite! Prehuman sounds!"

I could not hear the other side of the conversation, just Fraboni saying, "Sure. . . . Fine. . . . Great. . . . No problem! I will!"

When he hung up, he was smiling at me.

"You have tickets waiting for you at the airport," he said. "Your appointment with Mr. Blackwell is in London for tomorrow."

"Blackwell?" I repeated. "Would that be Chris Blackwell?"

"Yes, exactly. Chris in person."

I could not believe it. A meeting with the founder and president of Island Records, one of the most innovative and influential labels in popular music, with artists such as Bob Marley, U-2, and Melissa Etheridge, to name but a few. And now he wanted to hear my music of the spheres.

"So," my new friend said, rising. "Let me know how things work out with you and Chris."

And with that he left me standing in the doorway of Studio B with my head spinning.

As an astronomer, I live in two radically different universes of time. One moment I am sitting in a computer laboratory examining a celestial object that might have ceased to exist millions of years ago. And the next moment I am sitting in my car, drumming my fingers on the steering wheel because the traffic light seems to be taking an eternity to change. Cosmic time and human time—it is hard to conceive that they both exist in the same dimension. But soon I was sitting on an airplane with a cassette of sounds captured from as long ago as the Jurassic Age, headed for a London meeting with a music executive . . . because a day earlier someone across the hall had spent five minutes listening to this tape and loved it.

Chris Blackwell is a nice-looking Englishman with an unprepossessing manner. He ushered me into his office and immediately began playing short takes of music from a variety of artists he was thinking of signing. After each cut, he asked my opinion. They all sounded very good and professional to me. Finally, he leaned across his desk and asked me about my own music.

For reasons that to this day I do not fully understand, I immediately launched into a detailed account of my techniques in Acoustic Astronomy, transforming radio waves into sound. I kept pulling graphs and diagrams from my hastily packed bag, laying them out on Blackwell's desk, pointing, chattering nervously—talking about everything but music. After several minutes, he held up his hand and said, "Can I play the tape?"

I pulled my cassette from my bag and handed it to him. He slipped it into his stereo, leaned back in his chair, and listened to the 180-million-year-old sounds for approximately two minutes. Then he stopped the tape, popped it out, handed it back to me, and stood, saying that it had been a pleasure to meet me. That was it. He did not say another word! Not a single word about what he had just heard. The meeting was over.

Time to fly back to Milan and prepare my physics lesson for Monday morning.

On my flight home, the events of the day looped over and over in my mind. I could not believe how I had acted. Why had I chosen to behave like a student with this powerful music executive? What in heaven's name had that astronomy lecture been all about? Merely nervousness? Did I really think I could break into entertainment by proving what an accomplished astrophysicist I was? I had not even played Mr. Blackwell my own compositions—my jamming with the Cosmos—only the raw radio translations I had captured at the university. In a word, I had blown it.

Months passed. Not a word from Island Records. I tried to put the whole episode behind me. It was not meant to be, I told myself. The whole thing had been just a funny little weekend adventure. A surprise trip to London.

And then, almost a year to the day after that surprise trip, I received a phone call as precipitous and unexpected as that knock on the door of Studio B. It was Island asking for the name of my lawyer since my contract was ready. A few weeks later I was in New York City cutting my first album, tentatively titled *Music from the Galaxies.*

When the album was released a year later, a sticker on the cover of my Island CD announced that it was a "landmark release, an uncommon fusion of art and science, of music and astronomy." Since I wanted people to hear this raw data without any human alteration, the first six cuts of my CD were pure sounds from UGC 6697. The first cut, "Sidereal Breath," is almost eleven minutes of alternating sounds looped to resemble the long and deep respiration of the Cosmos; the second, "Galactic Beats," is an accelerating galactic drumroll; "Stellar Wind" is a vibrating tempest, like a gathering thunderstorm; "Plasma Waves" sounds like thick, undulating waves; "Collision" is exactly that, particles colliding at the speed of light; and "Radio Core" is the pulsating inner heart of the galaxy.

Only on the seventh cut, titled "Cosmic Time," did humanly produced music join with these sounds in the form of an arrangement for strings that I had composed. *Music from the Galaxies* is a timeless CD—it won't go out of date

Music from the Galaxies, Island Records CD
ARTWORK PROVIDED COURTESY OF ISLAND RECORDS, INC.

for at least 180 million years! Happily, the press was as enthralled by these otherworldly sounds as my private listeners had been; the reviews were ecstatic. Suddenly, I was back in the United States, touring colleges and universities from coast to coast as a self-invented hybrid Astrophysicist-slash-Musician.

Although I knew I would miss my students very much, I resigned from my teaching position at the Liceo—my classroom was expanding to include the whole world.

Pop Science

Coming out of the laboratory closet was not easy for me. The academic life is seductive in its security and elitism—it was hard for me to give up all that. As a scientist, I could have stature in my field and an assured job by simply doing what I had been trained to do—lecturing about the Doppler effect or redshifts or Max Planck's black body equation in a technical language that only my colleagues and a handful of students would understand. But I wanted people to experience and enjoy science in a new way. I wanted to inspire them and capture their hearts so that their learning would have an emotional home.

"Popular science"—what a sneering, derogatory term that is for so many people I have encountered: "bringing it down to their level," "reducing the complex to a simple common denominator," "trivializing the work of geniuses so that ordinary people can take it in."

These critics seem to believe that if more people understand a body of knowledge, the quality of that knowledge is necessarily cheapened. Actually, I feel it is the other way around—the quality of that knowledge is made much more valuable. Knowledge stimulates knowledge; ideas stimulate ideas. An "ordinary" person who has learned something about the Universe has a much deeper experience when she gazes up at the sky. And who knows where that deeper experience will lead?

I am proud to be a part of that growing group of people who are trying to rescue knowledge from the exclusivity of scientists. And I am particularly proud to be in the forefront of those scientists who are bringing art—and, yes, even entertainment—back into the world of science. They have been banished from that world for far too long.

Academic Striptease

A huge university auditorium. From the wings, I watch the seats fill, people overflowing into the aisles. I feel a familiar mix of excitement and nervousness as they settle in. They are waiting for me. . . .

I walk onstage covered from neck to knees in a starched white laboratory coat, my hair up in a tight bun. I even wear a pair of faux reading glasses to complete the image of the ultrasmart, no-nonsense professor. I stride to the blackboard and begin my lecture on galaxies and radio galaxies, using a laser pointer to mark the points as I make them . . . But within minutes, words and illustrations are not enough to say everything I want to communicate to this expectant audience. I want them to feel the excitement of exploring the Invisible Universe. The awe of flying through the Cosmos. I want the facts and theories that I have listed on the blackboard to come dynamically alive!

I pull on my shoulder-strap keyboard and begin to play "NEO," a song I co-wrote with Thomas Dolby for The Gate to the Mind's Eye. *It is a pulsing tune in which I sing about Near Earth Objects. As synthesized strings and a deep drum rhythm join me over the loudspeakers, I start to sing "Quantum Mechanic." Suddenly, this whole place is pulsating.*

Girls and boys, women and men rise from their seats all over the auditorium. They are dancing to "Quantum Mechanic." And now I am dancing, too. I loosen my hair, letting my blond tresses drop and swing to the music. I slip off my professional glasses and toss them to the wings.

Shimmying, I begin to unbutton my lab coat, one button at a time. The spotlight picks up the glint of the aluminum space collar I wear beneath it. Then the glistening silver of my plunging bodice, then the glow of my skin. Another but-

ton and my waist-hugging metallic corset is revealed. Another
button and my silver-gray miniskirt is exposed, its Saturn's
ring hoop undulating to the beat of the music. The lab coat
slides to my feet. Gone, done with. . . .

> *This is the new me! The real me——Divadoc!*
> *The audience roars.*

My showstopper, the Academic Striptease. In it, I re-
capitulate my personal evolution from Defeminized Scientist
to New Feminine Scientist, from Humorless Professional to
Fanciful Teacher, from Stern Lecturer to Cosmic Navigator,
from Material Girl to Galactic Girl. I am free——free to be
myself! And, along with me, I have freed everyone in the
auditorium to create their own models of how they want
to be, to reinvent themselves just as I have reinvented myself.

Nebula

Sound and noise,
Music and stars,
From the whole Universe, radiations and music,
Sounds and melodies
From the faraway galaxies,
Notes echoing in the wind,
Eternal voices

As the sound and frequencies ascend
And from the stars, the wish to talk,
The art of impulses.

The Universe is an everlasting music, a melody . . .
Faraway, into the primordial Universe,
Suns and planets, stars and galaxies,
World of light
As reflected fragments against the dark empty space.
I have seen nebulae and comets,
pulsars and quasars,
But for the very first time . . . I am hearing.

THE SEX LIFE
OF THE COSMOS

"Be my Comet and Take me to the Sky, Tonight!"

Binary People

I am gazing at Sirius A and Sirius B, a pair of binary stars that circle a common center of mass with a balance and precision so exact that you can set the Cosmic Clock by their alternating eclipses. They are held together by their mutual gravitational attraction—that is why neither one dominates the other, neither pulls its opposite off its analogous orbit or consumes it in its flaming gases. Each star has distinct properties, different surface brightness and temperature—a unique identity. These two have danced in unison for millions of years, each taking its solo turn while the other spins patiently in eclipse, awaiting visibility.

I remember once seeing some peasants dance a dance like this in Sicily—perfectly matched pairs of men and women circling each other in a steady rhythm, never taking their eyes off one another. It was a cheering sight for a

BINARY STAR

Sirius A is the brightest star appearing in the sky after our Sun. In classical mythology it was thought to be a dog that had changed into a star, and that is why it is also called the Dog Star, or Canicula. Its companion, *Sirius B*, is a White Dwarf with only 1/10,000 the luminosity of Sirius A. These two stars revolve around each other, moving around a common center of mass; they are kept together by a strong gravitational field.

Located approximately 8.8 light-years from Earth, this pair can be seen in the southern constellation of Canis Major.

Milanese girl who had grown up seeing the dances of sophisticated, urbane men and women—violent dances of power and submission, dances of false feelings, and dances of abandonment.

Behind Sirius A, I see the echoing, symmetrical rays of Sirius B as it begins to emerge from eclipse to take center celestial stage in its partner's place.

And what is this I feel as I peer over 8.8 light-years to these binary stars?

DR. FIORELLA TERENZI

My God, it is envy! Yes, I envy these two heavenly bodies their perfect harmony, their mutual respect, their eons of total devotion to one another, their synchronized eternal dialogue.

They are perfect lovers.

Having been a student for most of my young life, I have found that there are two basic ways to learn: by prescription and by modeling. In the first mode, the professor hands the student formulae and laws to commit to memory and to employ in problem solving; in the second, the student learns by example, by inspiration and analogy. I have always learned infinitely better in the latter way—the lessons are much more likely to take seed in my mind if they have first inspired my heart. My grandmother was the most inspiring teacher I ever had.

And when it comes to learning about the quirks and quandaries of the human heart, the ways of love and the complexities of sex, I have learned much more from gazing through my telescope at heavenly bodies like Sirius A and Sirius B than I ever learned from the prescriptions of my parents or those of the sisters at church and at school.

Of course, it takes some leaps of imagination to learn about love and sex from the stars. . . .

More than half the stars in the known Universe come in matched pairs, the binary stars. With numbers like that, maybe they are trying to tell us something. Take this pair I see in the lens of my telescope right now. They are, indeed, my idea of an ideal relationship: although Sirius A shines brighter in the sky than Sirius B, neither star dominates the other, neither makes itself subservient to the other; they give each other equal time in the cosmic spotlight. And this perfectly symmetrical dance of theirs, each simultaneously circling the other, makes me think of those rare moments when two partners making love are perfectly synchronized—each lover's caress and kiss, fondle and embrace, answered in flawless synchrony.

Oh God, that feeling of envy again!

It is not simply the *idea* of perfect synchrony that I find so enviably attractive here—it is the *feeling of its cosmic rightness, the sense of its being inherent to the Natural Order of things for two similar but distinct bodies to coexist in perfect harmony.*

This is a feeling that you can get only by peering out at space through a telescope.

Tale of a Galactic Gobbler

But there are warnings out there in the Cosmos, too—one in particular that I wish my dearest friend, Sophia, had heeded when she was a very young girl. . . .

At that time Sophia had a weakness for charming, attentive men who were strong, divine to look at, and loaded with self-confidence. Italy seems to specialize in producing these types. They prowl the cafés of Rome and Milan, seeking out impressionable young girls who have grown up in homes with strong, willful fathers and submissive Italian mothers, making us easy psychological prey for their machismo.

There was one in particular who nearly nebulized Sophia when she was only seventeen. His name was Alfredo and he was quite beautiful—tall, lean, with a magnificent leonine head covered with curly blue-black hair. His eyes alone were enough to grab her into his orbit; they were as dark and deep as a black hole, and she felt them on her before she even realized that he was sitting at the next table as she sat studying an opera score in her favorite café near the Conservatorio Giuseppe Verdi. She tried to ignore him, tried to keep her eyes glued to Puccini, but it was no use; his fiery stare ignited something in her. Finally, after what seemed like eons, she looked up and saw him smiling at her. And what a flashing smile it was—glittering white teeth set like a row of incandescent stars in a confident jaw.

"Ah, you are the perfect Mimi," he said, nodding at her score of *La Bohème*. "Frail and passionate. Are you performing here in Milan?"

She told him that she was only a student and tried to get back to her work, but all was lost—he had already seated himself at her table. And as he reached for the score in front of her, the back of his hand brushed against her forearm.

I repeat, she was only seventeen. How was she to know that he had practiced this move a thousand times, brushing the bare forearms of many young women before her?

They talked, they sang, they drank, they ate. Their affair began only days later. She was sure she loved him and never doubted for a moment that he adored her. Why should she? He told her constantly how much he loved her. (I often hear my American women friends complain that their husbands and lovers never use the "L" word. They should have an affair with an Italian man—the word *amore* pours out of his mouth like wine from a carafe. That would quickly cure my friends of their sense of verbal deprivation.)

How long did her affair with Alfredo go on? A million years? Two? Three?

She says that she cannot recall. But she does remember leaving the conservatory an hour early one evening and spotting Alfredo in that very same café, the back of his hand brushing against the forearm of an attractive woman perhaps a year younger than she. She stood silently just a few meters away, eclipsed from his view by a kiosk. "You are a perfect Mimi," he was crooning, his dark eyes flashing.

Yes, *nebulized* is the perfect word for what she felt at that moment. She felt as if she shattered into a billion particles, each shooting off in a different direction. She felt as if she would never feel whole again. But she slowly put herself back together with the aid of her anger.

It would take two more foolish romances such as that one before Sophia realized that something in *her*—in her own responses—needed to change. But what was it about the Alfredos of the world that always seemed to both attract her and blind her to their destructiveness?

It was by peering through my telescope that I finally found clues to the answer to Sophia's dilemma. . . .

I was gazing out across several million light-years at the galaxy ESO B138. Like the million-plus other galaxies within optical view of our largest telescopes, this one is made up of billions of stars as well as of gas and dust.

But I had recently discovered something distressing about this galaxy's dark past—its abusive relationship with a former lover.

Like most love affairs, ESO B138's relationship with IG 29/30 began innocently enough, with a charming flirtation. IG 29/30 was hovering a mere fifty million light-years away, close enough to capture ESO B138's attention, but not close enough to be caught up in his gravitational field.

Perhaps several million years passed before ESO B138 couldn't stand it any longer. He launched fiery flashes in IG 29/30's direction. Coquettishly, IG 29/30 ignored them. A

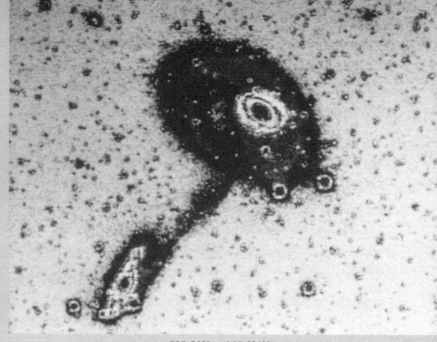

ESO B138 and IG 29/30

ESO B138 AND IG 29/30

Galaxies are composed of stars and gas, so when galaxies such as these nearly collide by mutual gravity, the stars and gas are disturbed. Here, a large amount of gas from one of the galaxies has been pulled into a streamer by the gravitational force of the other. This streamer is made up of gas that normally would not be visible, but now has been lit up by bright, newly born stars. As the galaxies move apart, most of the stars forming the streamer will fall back into the larger galaxy.

spiral galaxy, she twisted and gyred on her merry way, never coming any closer to ESO B138. But his fiery entreaties persisted—incandescent jets of flaming gases shot toward IG 29/30, then retreated back to their source, as if to say, "This way, my dear—follow the blazing path." No response. Again, he thrust a flaming jet toward her. And again she demurred.

Another several million years went by. Finally, ESO B138 launched a fiery missive that penetrated IG 29/30's gravitational field, passing through several million of her stars.

That did it. IG 29/30 began to gyrate toward him, very gradually at first, but after a few million years she was circling in his orbit.

Was it ESO B138's persistence over the multimillennia that had done it? Was it IG 29/30's loneliness, sailing around solo in an envelope of black space?

Or was it ESO B138's incandescent display of sheer power that finally captured her?

IG 29/30 circled the larger ESO B138 for several million years in seeming harmony. Yes, ESO B138 was bigger and more beautiful than IG 29/30. And, indeed, IG 29/30 was completely in ESO B138's power, locked into orbit in his grand gravitational field. Yet it seemed to work. They shared light and energy, and, most important, they had followed the Law of Nature that gathers bodies together in the infinite black void.

But then it happened—ESO B138 became restless. He felt dissatisfied with only one galaxy orbiting him, and he shot a jet of fire at another distant galaxy that had caught his eye. And when IG 29/30 resisted sharing her orbital space with this galactic interloper, ESO B138 became violent. He focused his gravitational pull onto her and drew her to him.

That was the end, of course. IG 29/30 lost her identity and her independence. Her destiny was set: swallowed up by ESO B138 over millions of years.

Gazing through my giant telescope, I could envision the faint line that would remain in space showing where she once existed, like the soft imprint left on the pillow by a departed lover.

That night, as I logged out and turned off the lights in the observatory, I found myself thinking about Sophia and how foolish she had been to be so dazzled by Alfredo's incandescent flares and relentless flattery. And suddenly I had an insight so personally profound, yet also so simple and obvious, that I knew right then and there that once I told Sophia about it there would be no more Alfredos haunting her life. *I had finally understood that, like ESO B138, Alfredo had incredible powers of attraction that were identical to his powers of destruction.* Indeed, the very qualities that had pulled Sophia into Alfredo's magnetic field—his self-assurance, his personal beauty, his impulsive passion—*were the very qualities that ultimately destroyed her and all the other young women who were drawn into his orbit.*

Along with Alfredo's self-assurance came his amorality—he was so confident in his own rightness that he felt he could do anything with impunity, including being unfaithful. Along with Alfredo's beauty came his vanity—he came to need the flattering responses of ever-new conquests. And along with his impulsive passion came his disloyalty—his impulsiveness was license for faithlessness. These properties were as immutable as any Law of Nature. Clearly, it was my friend who had to change if she were ever to find satisfying love in her life.

This lesson came to me literally like a gift from the heavens.

The Dead-End Love of M87 and M84

Tonight another sad galactic love story slides into focus in my telescope's lens. There seems to be no end to them. . . .

Just yesterday, my friend Paula confided to me that she was thinking of leaving her lover, Erik, but she was torn and unsure.

"I have invested so much in this relationship already," she told me. "But I'm getting older and he still says he isn't ready to make a total commitment. But on the other hand, if I leave him now, I'll have to start all over again with someone else—and who knows if that relationship would go any better anyhow?"

I didn't know what to advise my friend. . . .

I am peering at the Virgo Cluster of galaxies. At its center is a glowing fuzzy globe that appears innocuous enough, but I know that what I am observing is one of the most massive galaxies in the known Universe. It is the giant elliptical galaxy known to astronomers as M87 (though I have renamed him Rex Narcissus). This galaxy is the gravitational center of the great Virgo Cluster in the constellation Virgo.

Rex lies there like a self-satisfied sovereign at the center of his family of galaxies, surrounded by fifteen thousand globular clusters, spherical clusters of a hundred thousand to a million stars each. And encircling them all is a cloud of gas with a mass equal to one trillion Suns and a temperature of thirty million degrees Kelvin.

Now, lying silently next to Rex is one of the other prominent members of the Virgo Cluster, known to astronomers as M84 (to me, as Virgo Dolores). Although Dolores was originally thought to be a classical elliptical galaxy, recent discoveries suggest that she is lenticular (shaped like a lentil, or a double convex lens), surrounded by a flattened disk of stars. This is significant in that if Dolores does indeed possess the dust and gas clouds necessary for forming new stars, she may

M87

NATIONAL OPTICAL ASTRONOMY OBSERVATORIES

M 8 7

This innocuous-appearing fuzzy globe is, in fact, one of the most massive galaxies known in the Universe, containing over a trillion stars. It is the giant elliptical galaxy known as M87, the gravitational center of the great Virgo Cluster in the constellation Virgo.

The mass statistics for this galaxy are staggering. It is surrounded by 15,000 globular clusters, spherical clusters of 100,000 to 1 million stars each, compared with a mere 130 for our own Milky Way. The jet of light you see protruding from one side of the galaxy is a hot stream of ionized gas ejected at enormous speed from the core of the galaxy. Measurements indicate the gas is moving at tens of thousands of kilometers per second.

M87 and its jet have provided the first hard evidence of one of the most peculiar objects in the universe—a supermassive black hole with enough matter to create 3 billion Suns!

Virgo Cluster of Galaxies
NATIONAL OPTICAL ASTRONOMY OBSERVATORIES

THE VIRGO CLUSTER

Thousands of galaxies swarm like bees in this optical image of the great gathering of galaxies in the constellation Virgo known as the Virgo Cluster. By intergalactic standards, the Virgo Cluster is a next-door neighbor, its center lying only about 70 million light-years away.

Indeed, it is so "near" that our own galaxy, the Milky Way, is believed to be part of a larger system to which both it and the Virgo Cluster belong.

Clusters of galaxies like this one are a link in the great chain of organization of matter in the Universe. Thus, billions of stars are bound together by gravity into galaxies. Gravity, in turn, binds small numbers of galaxies into groups of twenty to thirty. Groups and isolated galaxies are in turn bound by gravity into clusters like the Virgo Cluster, consisting of thousands of galaxies.

M84

NATIONAL OPTICAL ASTRONOMY OBSERVATORIES

M 8 4

One of the most prominent members of the Virgo Cluster, the galaxy M84 is seen in this visible light image. Originally thought to be a classic elliptical galaxy, M84 is now believed to be lenticular—an elliptical core surrounded by a flattened disk of stars. The classification is significant: once thought to be almost completely lacking in the gas and dust clouds required to form new stars, as is typical of elliptical galaxies, M84 has been found in recent observations to have a small but measurable amount of such clouds. Nevertheless, its approximately 500 billion stars appear quite old, implying that its glory days of intense star formation are long past.

still be fertile after all. But her progeny of 500 billion stars appear relatively old, suggesting that Dolores's most fruitful years are behind her.

So now she just lies there, virtually ignored by Rex Narcissus, who neither consumes her nor lets her go, but just keeps her dangling in his gravitational field as she grows older by the millennium.

"Let go!" I sigh to myself. "This relationship is going nowhere! Before you know it, you will not have another star left in you to be born! Break the tie! Sail on! There are millions of galaxies out in space who would treat you with more respect! Who would give you the attention you deserve! If you do not have the faith in yourself to chart your own course, you will languish in his gravitational field for the rest of your life. Take the risk. You have nothing to lose but your dependency."

I could not wait to phone Paula to offer her the celestial perspective on her relationship with Erik. I told her this galactic story of dead-end love, of a heavenly body who gives everything to her lover and gets nothing in return except another millennium older.

"It is the cosmic embodiment of that eternal lover's mistake—hanging on to a relationship long after it is over," I said. "You are suffering from galactic inertia. You feel that you've invested so many years in this relationship you can't sail off and start anew somewhere else. But it is just because you have been there so long—languished for so long—that you have to make the break right now!''

"There you go again, Fiorella''—my friend laughed—"turning the Universe into a lovelorn column.''

Nonetheless, by the time our conversation ended, Paula felt strong and inspired enough to finally break her tie with Eric.

"You see,'' she said, "I still have all these lovely stars inside me just waiting to be born.''

Of Mice and Men

I recently saw an article in a journal of neurophysiology that brought a guilty smile to my face. It seems that a team of neuroanatomists had isolated a locus in the monkey brain where orgasms are produced—or at least where the *sensation* of an orgasm is generated. By sending a low-level electrical current to this spot, the experimenters were able to keep the monkey in orgasmic ecstasy for as long as they wanted. They concluded that it would be possible to locate and stimulate the same spot in the human brain.

Of course, like anyone else with a bit of imagination, I found myself wondering what it would be like to be hooked up to such a neurostimulator and to spend the rest of my days (and nights) in perpetual climax. After all, isn't maximizing bliss the ultimate goal of life? Don't we all put up with the routines and hard work of daily life just so we can experience those rare ecstatic moments? Is there anything in our lives that even begins to compare with the joys and thrills of sensuality? Freud had it right when he said that we all operate on the pleasure principle.

Or did he? Faced with the technological possibility of perpetual orgasm, I seriously doubted if that would really be a satisfying way to live. Would perpetual pleasure mean anything to me without something to compare it with?

This was not the first time I had asked myself these questions.

I remember one period in my life when I was on a marathon schedule of astronomical research. I was glued to my computer for up to twenty hours a day sorting data for a paper I was writing about radio galaxies. Now and then, I would catnap on a cot right there at the university, but then I would be up again and at my computer, ready to record my next observations. During this phase, I obviously had no time for diversions of any kind, certainly not for romance.

But like the naughty schoolgirl I in part will forever be, every once in a while I would turn my attention from Coma Berenices to recall on the computer monitor the delightfully sexy pair of galaxies known as the Mice. For the life of me, I cannot gaze at these two without perceiving them as locked in an erotic embrace, forever contracting and expanding into one another. As a rule, when two galaxies are in relatively close proximity each gives off a separate and distinct radiance, but together this undulating couple gives off a single, spectacularly luminous glow that outshines all other galactic pairs. It is, I am convinced, the glow of mutual ecstasy. And these two have been at it for several million years.

Whenever I would sneak these glimpses at the Mice, I would feel a little ripple of sensuality pass through my exhausted body, so tense from concentration, so devoid of any feeling except constant tension without release. And inevitably, I would long for a purely sensual existence like this galactic pair, forever pleasuring each other. At those particular moments, there was no question in my mind that perpetual ecstasy was far preferable to no ecstasy at all.

I remember that when I first observed this galactic pair I asked the professor what their ultimate fate would be and he answered with a shrug, "Oh, in a few million years they will finally consume each other."

Oh yes, but what a way to go. . . .

The Excommunicated Nebula

"Did you touch yourself?" the priest asked me through the mahogany filigree of the confessional.

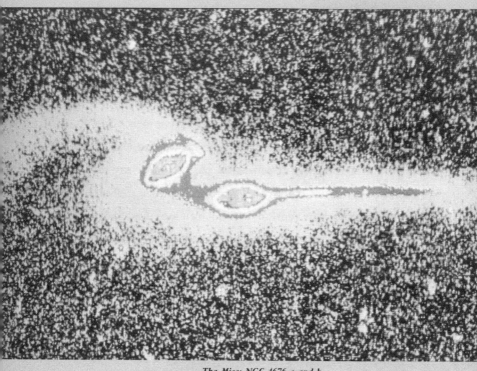

The Mice: NGC 4676 a and b
NATIONAL OPTICAL ASTRONOMY OBSERVATORIES

THE MICE:
NGC 4676 A AND B

The Mice are playing! These two galaxies, known as the Mice, are undergoing a strong interaction. As a result of their close encounter, streams of gas have been pulled from each galaxy.

I was eight years old and had not the slightest idea what he was talking about.

"I don't know," I answered hesitantly. "I mean, I touch myself when I wash my face and when I scratch a mosquito bite. Is that what you mean, Father?"

"No, that is *not* what I mean, child!" the priest retorted severely.

I left confession puzzled and vaguely guilty. Had I done something evil that I had not reported to him? Or worse, had I done something that I didn't even realize was evil, but nonetheless would be punished for in the hereafter? I asked my mother, who embarrassedly walked away. I asked my sister, who was as baffled as I was.

"Did you touch yourself?" the priest inquired the moment I seated myself at my next confession.

"I don't think so," I replied. "May I ask, Father, what it means to touch yourself?"

"You know very well what I mean," he replied, and went on to inquire about how my catechism was progressing.

This enigmatic colloquy continued for the next few years of my life, and then, when I was twelve, a new, even more urgent question was added: "Did anyone touch you?"

Finally it all started to make sense to me. After all, I lived not only in a repressive Catholic culture but also in a culture that celebrated sensuality in all its various forms, from food to couture, and a culture that for centuries had been in love with the beauty of the female body. What is more, I had just begun to blossom as a young woman, to feel the first glimmer of sexual sensation awakening in my own body.

"No, no one has touched me," I replied to the priest. I put a transparent hint of disappointment in my voice when I said this, but I am sure that this is as defiant as I dared to be at that point in my life. Of one thing I am certain, however: At the age of twelve I already suspected that the priests were the ones who were most obsessed with sex.

The holy battle against sexuality continued in my life. We girls were warned by the sisters never to look at our bodies in a mirror, never to wear tight-fitting or revealing clothing, never to call attention to ourselves, never to arouse a man in any way.

"How can I tell if something I do arouses a man?" I asked one of the sisters, although at this point I already knew what the answer would be. *Anything* a woman did that had the effect of arousing a man, whether it was done intentionally or unintentionally, seductively or innocently, was evil. There was nothing remotely subtle about this message: The body of a woman, especially an attractive woman, was sinful. It was unnatural to think of your body as a source of pleasure for anyone—and that included yourself.

The young women in my neighborhood dealt with this

message in different ways. Some internalized it completely and ultimately took one of the two options left to them: They either became nuns themselves or married young and began producing children immediately. Others rebelled against the message with a vengeance that brought only misery into their lives. They became prostitutes or—worse, to my mind—became mistresses of churchgoing men who thought of their faithful wives as saints. Only a handful of us found a path where we could own our sexuality without degrading ourselves. And for my part, I owe my sexual salvation to both my love of opera and my love of the stars.

I was thirteen when I first saw Bizet's *Carmen*. I stumbled out of the opera house totally enthralled by both the music and the spirit of this masterpiece. Although I was only an adolescent (or perhaps *because* I was only an adolescent), I saw immediately that this play was about the eternal power struggle between men and women, that Don Carlos in his military officer's uniform was a symbol of masculine power, and that Carmen—poor, beautiful, and pulsating with lyrical sensuality—was a symbol of the only real power a woman could have over a man—sexual power. But the opera takes this struggle to its inevitable and tragic conclusion. Carmen refuses to allow her sexuality to be tamed, and Don Carlos, threatened to the very core by her sexual power over him, finally murders her. Some people like to say that it was a crime of passion, but I knew better: it was a crime of ultimate masculine power over the one thing he cannot completely control—a woman's sexual attractiveness. In the years that followed, *Carmen* helped me understand what my priest's obsession (as well as all male repression of female sexuality) was about—power and control.

Not long ago, after witnessing one of my lecture/performances, in which I enter the stage wearing a lab coat and spectacles and dance off an hour and a half later wearing my gossamer Saturn's moons gown with a synthesizer keyboard slung over my bare shoulder, a friend of mine exclaimed, "My God, Fiorella! You are the Carmen of astrophysics!"

My friend had no idea what a wonderful compliment this was. Nor did he realize that I am always on guard against repressive male physics professors carrying metaphoric daggers in their briefcases.

And how did the stars save me from the repressions that were drilled into me night and day by the nuns and priests?

I am gazing out at one of the most vivid, bright, and enchanting nebulae in the firmament. Her name is Helix Nebula, and she emits an incredibly colorful ring—a halo.

To me, that halo represented a process many of us know. She had to release all of her accumulated repression to move to the next stage in her cosmic life. She had to release all of her conditioning to expel it into that surrounding space.

DR. FIORELLA TERENZI

Helix Nebula
NATIONAL OPTICAL ASTRONOMY OBSERVATORIES

THE HELIX NEBULA

A cloud of gas that has been ejected by a dying star, the Helix Nebula is about 460 light-years away from the Earth in the Southern Hemisphere constellation of Aquarius. It has the largest apparent diameter of any planetary nebula, but despite its size it is too faint to be seen by the naked eye.

That halo of gas surrounding her central star speaks to me of
her new fulfilled nature. Her wonderful new glow is a halo of
satisfaction, a glow of self-esteem, of pride in who she is,
even a glow of pleasure, sensual pleasure—and that pleasure
could have no source other than herself. She needs no other
for satisfaction and she was not in the least ashamed of that.

But what would the priests say? Surely, they would be
scandalized. Without a doubt Helix would be excommunicated.

Goddess and God love you, Helix Nebula—sail on
through the Universe in total pleasure!

Be My Comet Tonight

When I meditate on the relationship between power and
sexual attraction, I can think of no more potent example
than that most masculine, most seductive, and most poten-
tially violent of heavenly bodies, the comet.

Recently, I had the opportunity to view via infrared
imaging the appearance of a glorious comet named (after its
human discoverers) Shoemaker-Levy 9. Like all comets, it
is made of ice and dust, and while it hurtles through space
all kinds of matter adhere to its surface, including dust particles and free-floating amino acids, the protein building
blocks of organic life. It is widely believed that it was a
comet-created crater filled with water and comet-borne
amino acids that gave Planet Earth both its oceans and its

first forms of single-cell life, from which all of us beguiled and befeathered four-legged and two-legged creatures are descended.

It is not a big stretch to think of a comet as a cosmic spermatozoon swimming through space with a forceful trajectory until it finds fertile territory in which to deposit itself.

But, of course, a comet also may arrive on the scene bearing Death. Some theories suggest that the Age of the Dinosaurs came to an abrupt end due to the impact of a comet or a giant meteorite. As well, the impact of a comet could cause a heavenly body to change rotation, even to wobble off course and disappear into the void.

As I gaze now at the infrared glow of Shoemaker-Levy 9, I find myself thinking about all the loves I have had that I shouldn't have. And all the loves that I might have had but didn't.

At this particular moment, the ways of love strike me as arbitrary, despite all my desire to believe that there is a purpose to everything, a Cosmic Order that defines each event in our lives.

Why was this particular comet grabbed by the gravitation of our Sun? It was not simply Shoemaker-Levy 9's mass. Greater comets have eluded the Sun's pull. No, it was a myriad of incalculable accidents of trajectory and velocity and the

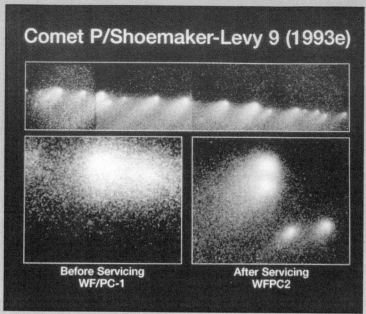

Shoemaker-Levy 9 Comet
NASA

SHOEMAKER-LEVY 9 COMET

The summer of 1994 saw what may be remembered as the most stupendous solar system event of this century—or even possibly of this millennium. For the first time in recorded history, a comet was observed colliding with a planet—Jupiter. Starting on July 16, Shoemaker-Levy 9 began a six-day-long sequence of impacts that were observed by both amateur and professional astronomers all across the globe.

The final results turned out to be more phenomenal than anyone had expected or even hoped. In this Hubble Space Telescope image we can clearly see the tremendous dark patches produced by the collisions.

HISTORY

Unknown to astronomers at the time, this spectacular event actually began on July 7, 1992, when a then-undiscovered comet made a very close pass by Jupiter, the largest planet in the solar system. In this near miss the planet's gravity fragmented the icy core of the comet into many pieces. This unusual comet was discovered nearly a year later, on March 24, 1993, by the comet-hunting trio Eugene and Carolyn Shoemaker and David Levy. Thereafter known as Shoemaker-Levy 9, the comet gained a special significance when astronomers realized that a year later it would return and actually hit Jupiter.

relative placement of things in the Milky Way at one particular instant in time. In short, it was being at the right place at the right time.

How many men have passed me by in the cafés of Milan, on the avenues of New York, in the clubs of L.A., and nothing at all happened. No response, no recognition, not so much as a glance of attraction.

Wrong trajectory. Wrong velocity. Wrong time of day.

And then one evening I am asked to open a Los Angeles music festival called the Festival of the Five Senses. It is a

Andromeda Galaxy
JPL/NASA

THE ANDROMEDA GALAXY

The Andromeda Galaxy (a.k.a. M31 or NGC 224) is an enormous spiral galaxy located a mere 2 million light-years from us. Although hard to see from a light-polluted city, Andromeda is the brightest galaxy visible in the Northern Hemisphere. It is estimated to be twice as massive as our own galaxy, the Milky Way—some pictures show it sprawling 157,000 light-years in length.

rainy night, but at curtain time it is standing room only. When I step out onto the stage, I again feel that thrill of a roaring crowd. When the noise dies down, I tell them that tonight I will take them on a cruise to the outer limits of the Universe.

I start by taking them to the Andromeda Galaxy, an enormous spiral galaxy a mere 2 million light-years away from us. On the huge screen behind me, I appear in a long red dress, draped over Andromeda, that hazy river of light we can see running across the sky on a clear night. I tell them what we can learn about our own galaxy, the Milky Way, by observing Andromeda.

But now the crowd is calling for music. They want to hear me sing with the Cosmos. I grab my keyboard and start to jam with the galaxies, the radio astronomical sounds that I recorded in the observatory. I find myself in the thrall of the most sensual, primordial galactic solo I have ever done. I *am* the Orbital Mind that I am singing about. I am floating above Planet Earth, looking down with joy and compassion.

The crowd cheers on as I go from one song to the next. They are skyrocketing with me. They are breathing in synchronization with our Cosmos. And when I finally finish, the applause is deafening.

I return to my dressing room, floating ever so gradually back to Earth. And then the organizer of the festival knocks at my door and asks if she may introduce me to someone who loved my performance. When I say yes and he steps through the door of my dressing room, the instant attraction between us is as real and powerful as if it had been obeying Newton's Third Law of Dynamics—the mutual attraction of bodies. He wants me to fly to the stars with him, and I say, Yes, of course, because at the moment there is no other possible answer. Because he is my comet.

Why this man at this time when so many others—many of them handsome and powerful and intelligent—have passed so close to me without a flicker of attraction between us?

The answer is simple: *Right trajectory. Right velocity. Right time of day. . . .*

Harmony and Discordance. Attraction and Destruction. Inertia and Regeneration. Pleasure and Pain. Independence and Dependence. Cosmic Order and Cosmic Chaos. These polarities have always found their way into every human cosmology and into every analysis of human relationships, dating back to the days of the goddesses.

Could that be because in every time and place some philosophical thinker lifted her eyes to the night sky?

THE HUMAN STAR POPULATION: A HILLSIDE MEDITATION

*"Let me be a superb supernova! Let me
explode with each single atom in a
magnificent glow of glory!"*

The Shining and the Shined-Upon

*The night sky, so silent, so deep. It envelops me like a velvet
lover. It transports me back in time to when my ancestors
assigned names of gods with human traits to the planets and
constellations that they beheld: "That reddish orange ball
hovering near the Moon, so fiery and aggressive-looking—we
shall call it Mars, god of war. And that enchanting, softly
luminous globe, the first we see at nightfall—that shall be
Venus, the paragon of feminine beauty . . ."*

I am back in my favorite astronomical observatory—the country hillside near my grandmother's farm outside of Milan. More than twenty years have passed since that first ecstatic moment when my grandmother introduced me to the Stellar Heart. I lie here in the grass with my eyes straight up to the stars, letting my imagination soar as I gaze at the celestial drama unfolding above me.

Once again, I am bewitched by the thought that these heavenly bodies possess human characteristics, that they can convey lessons and warnings to us here on Earth.

Perhaps the most fundamental categories we use for dividing the celestial population are Objects That Produce Their Own Light and Objects That Only Reflect Light, the Shining and the Shined-Upon. In the first category are all the objects that burn their own interior fuel, preeminently stars, as well as all the objects that burn from the friction they create as they race through gases, like meteorites ignited by friction with our atmosphere. And in the second category are all the heavenly bodies that bathe in the light transmitted to them.

It would be easy to claim that the objects that produce their own light are the heroines and heroes of the firmament—they are the self-starters, dependent on no one but themselves for energy, for their very existence. In the human population, they remind us of the great innovators and luminaries—the Da Vincis and Marconis, the

Curies and Edisons, the Plancks and Einsteins. These men and women ignited themselves; they drew on their own inner resources to create something new and previously unimaginable. Standing among those who did not produce their own light, they shone. As if in testimony to their greatness, these self-generating heavenly bodies are surrounded by lesser, nonluminous objects that orbit them like acolytes.

But lying here on the hillside in the dead of night, I am smiling because I know there is so much more to the story than simply the Shining and the Shined-Upon, the heroes and the acolytes.

The synergy between these two kinds of celestial objects is one of the primary miracles of the Universe. We on Earth, the Shined-Upon, are in the thrall of our great shining star, the Sun; we are eternally dependent on it for our energy, for all the life that blooms and swims and walks on our surface. But it is also true that this life could never arise on a burning object, not on any star. Not a single life-building molecule could survive on the Sun with its surface temperature of 5,800 degrees Kelvin. The miracle of organic life requires us, the Shined-Upon—our cool, unkindled surface, our fertile incubating waters, our steady, ever-

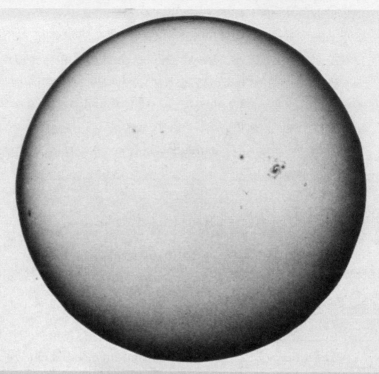

The Sun
NATIONAL OPTICAL ASTRONOMY OBSERVATORIES

THE SUN

Here you see in visible light the object that is, paradoxically, the most extraordinary object in our sky and, at the same time, one of the most ordinary astronomical objects: *the Sun.* For the Earth, the Sun is by far the brightest object in the sky, being nearly a million times brighter than the full Moon, which we can see only because it dimly reflects the Sun's light. It is the only source of radiation capable of transmitting the heat and energy necessary for life to exist on Earth. Without the Sun, life, human or otherwise, would be impossible here.

dependable circuit, neither too dangerously close nor too dangerously far from the burning Sun.

For me, the lesson here is simple, though nonetheless always important to be reminded of: *Every role is important. We are all in the same game and we are all dependent on one another.*

But there is another lesson for me in all of this, one that easily escapes my consciousness in my daily wanderings on Planet Earth. And that is: *Do not be blinded by the shining light of a star. It may be hiding a deeper truth about a relationship.*

I am thinking of a couple I know, two men who have been together for fifteen years. Kenneth is clearly the star of this pair—he is an immensely successful film actor, witty, graceful, and extraordinarily handsome. His partner, Philip, is a few years older, balding, awkward, and shy. Whenever the two of them appear at a party or in a restaurant, everyone's attention is instantly drawn to Kenneth and to Kenneth alone; if Philip were to abruptly disappear, his absence would barely register. I have even heard some friends say they feel sorry for Kenneth because he has to be burdened with this lackluster person forever orbiting him. But the truth is that in the drama of their daily lives Kenneth is every bit as dependent on Philip as Philip is dependent on Kenneth. I know them in their less public lives, and it is there that Kenneth's insecurities, intellectual lapses, and mood swings are all kept in check by Philip's dependable equilibrium. Philip is Kenneth's ballast, his secure home base, the person who makes it possible for him to be the witty and graceful charmer in public. So it goes with many couples I know. Yet how easy it is to be oblivious to this mutual dependence when you observe them only in the star's blinding light.

Interplanetary Travelers

Raising my head from the grass, I peer down at the border of the field where the night sky meets the tree line—the same tree line that marked the boundary of where I was allowed to play as a child.

Though I know that everything Out There is in constant motion, the night feels as still as a photograph. . . .

Floating around the solar system in rivers of particles, pieces of rock, comets and asteroids are those anonymous interplanetary travelers collectively known as Near Earth Objects (NEOs).

Some drift aimlessly. The heavens are heavily populated with such bits and pieces of matter that seem to be swept up in whatever orbital current they come into contact with, adding themselves to one or another current of space flotsam. Whenever I peer through a telescope and such a river comes into view, I think about all the people on Earth who are floaters, too, who passively drift in the river of life. They follow a set itinerary, a steady velocity—never accelerating or decelerating, never stopping to wonder what direction they are going in. *Is this the destination I really desire?*

They float on, from home to work and work to home. They could easily be led anywhere, to do anything. Like their celestial counterparts, they seldom encounter any friction or collision, going with the flow, yet never shining brightly, never leaving a luminous trail in the darkness.

But through my telescope I also see NEOs that seem to relish change. Floating close to the gravitational pull of Earth and its atmosphere, they suddenly abandon their aimless ways and fire themselves toward our planet.

There! Look, a sudden flash! It lasts no longer than it takes me to draw in my breath. A blazing meteor dives toward the horizon, burning out just before it disappears behind the trees.

Over 20 million meteors enter the Earth's atmosphere each day. Made up of small particles that swarm around the Sun, they are among the shortest-lived members of the Shined-Upon. The moment they drift into the Earth's upper atmosphere and begin rubbing against air particles, they create a fiery friction. Descending to the Earth's surface at forty-five miles per second, most of them ignite and destroy themselves in the blink of an eye. Yet for that brief space of time, they are gloriously visible . . . while their sister particles that have not been so intimately embraced by the Earth's pull continue to swarm invisibly.

For these NEOs, there is but one choice: to burn out in the bright light of fiery passion. In an instant, they exhaust their entire mass, all their potential—but in that instant, for the first and only time in their existence, they become visible.

When I was a teenager, my friends and I used to endlessly discuss the moral of the story of the moth and the flame. Attracted by the light and warmth of the flame, the moth flies so close that its powdery wings kindle, and in one white moment it is gone. The romantics among us— and even then that was most of us—were positive that it was worth it; one incomparable moment of white light and passionate heat was absolutely worth dying for. Whatever the outcome—success or failure—the inspiration that ignites will always leave its trace in the sky. I believe there will always be moments driven by meaningful goals when all caution should be abandoned for the sake of the flame. Is there not a part of all of us that longs for a moment of sublime brilliance? That longs to leave a meteoric streak in the sky?

But there are also those rare meteors that do not completely exhaust themselves in their fall toward Earth—the meteorites that land on our surface with terrific force. These can be forces of incredible *destruction*, but they can also be sources of terrific *instruction*—the craters they leave are mines of galactic chemical information. Like the heroines and heroes of classic mythologies, these rare NEOs have an impact that lasts much longer than a flash in the sky.

Often, meteorites make me think of the millions of spermatozoa that float in that female river of life known as the fallopian tubes: few make it near to the egg, and only one in millions fertilizes the egg, creating new life—possibly the most heroic journey of them all!

"Great is the gate and narrow is the way which leadeth to life, and few there will be who find it," Jesus said.

Galactic Cores, Hidden Hearts

My gaze drifts to a long swipe of white in the night sky like a floating silk scarf that half covers a goddess's naked torso. This is what the unassisted eye can see of the nearby swirl of our own galaxy, the Milky Way.

Even with the most sophisticated optical equipment, much of this galaxy's nucleus remains invisible to us, hidden, cloaked in the cosmic dust that swirls in the vast areas between the stars. For every trillion optical photons that are emitted from the galactic core, only one makes it out to visi-

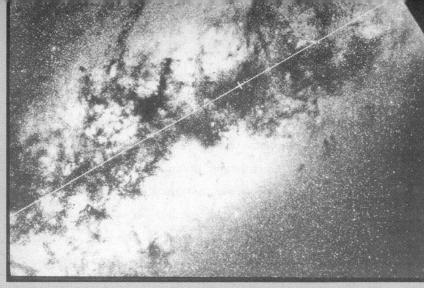

The Galactic Center

THE GALACTIC CENTER

Trying to see what our galaxy looks like is somewhat like trying to see yourself when you do not have a mirror—namely, a problem! You can see your own arms and legs, but not your face and back. It's a safe bet, though, that your back and head resemble those of other people. Similarly, we can see parts of our own Milky Way, but it is easier to trace its features—like its spiral arms and central bulge—after we have seen them in other galaxies. Seeing into the center of our own galaxy is especially difficult due to the enormous amounts of dust that lie in the vast areas between the stars.

The *Galactic Center* lies in the same area of sky as the constellation Sagittarius. This wide-angle view taken in the direction of the Galactic Center shows the Milky Way's central bulge as a blob of light. Notice how the bulge doesn't appear perfectly round; the light flattens out into a disklike shape. We can also see the dark outline of the dust belt (or dust lane), similar to the belt in Centaurus A.

bility from Earth—the other 999,999,999,999 all get ab-
sorbed by this dust.

We can make only educated guesses about the exact na-
ture of the galactic core. It appears to have an active nucleus
producing prodigious amounts of energy. It may even contain
a gigantic black hole with a mass a million times that of the
Sun. For now, it remains an enticing mystery. . . .

Lena was the first friend I made in Los Angeles, and
she remains my closest friend. Such an enduring friendship
is no small accomplishment. Lena is a young woman of such
incredible beauty that I have seen an entire city street come
to a halt when she stepped outside—cars stopped and men
abruptly turned in their tracks, registering a mix of desire
and wonder . . . all of this in Los Angeles, America's mag-
net for the most beautiful women in the world. In other
words, Lena emits a strong gravitational field.

Whenever Lena and I go out for dinner, whether we
go to a local diner or to one of Hollywood's famous res-
taurants for the Shining, men approach her the moment we
enter. They slip her their business cards, invite her to ex-
clusive parties, and make her on-the-spot offers to appear
in their shows or films. The evening usually ends with one
of them proposing a weekend in Paris or Hawaii. According
to Lena, she has had this effect on people since she was a
young girl, and nothing she tries to do to hide her beauty—

even wearing sweatpants, sneakers, and a baggy sweater—alters that effect. I know that this woman is very much more than simply what the eye can see. But at her core, in her innermost heart, Lena is a prisoner of her overwhelming attractiveness.

She is afraid that everything people say and do is part of a plot to possess her. She does not even trust those men who gaze sincerely into her lavender eyes and ask her to talk about herself—she is sure it is just another ploy. In defense, Lena covers her heart completely, reveals nothing. She plays the role of the tough, sexy bombshell to the hilt, toying with men but never becoming genuinely intimate. Her galactic core is covered with dust that does not allow her to shine as she should. In the end, she feels very much alone.

So, to the Shining and the Shined-Upon, we must add another category of human-star subjects: those whose inner light never escapes—the Hidden Hearts.

As I look up at the wispy trail of the Milky Way, I wonder how much of my own galactic core remains hidden. How much of it is covered by the swirling dust of my insecurities? How much is obscured by my fear of not meeting the expectations of others?

Suddenly, an earthly cloud blows overhead, momentarily obscuring everything—moon, stars, Venus, Mars. And it oc-

The Milky Way Galaxy
NATIONAL OPTICAL ASTRONOMY OBSERVATORIES

THE MILKY WAY GALAXY

If you look up at the sky on a clear night, you'll notice a hazy river of light running clear across the sky. You are seeing more than 100 billion stars. This is our galactic home—the *Milky Way*.

When seen in profile, the Milky Way Galaxy looks like a pancake with a fat middle. On the outside edges of the entire galaxy lies a halo of old stars and globular star clusters that formed when the galaxy was still very young. Because there is no gas in this halo, no new stars can be generated. The middle part of the disk is thinly populated with stars and star-forming clouds of dust and gas. In the central region, however, stars, dust, and gas are so highly concentrated that they obscure our view of one of the most intriguing regions of our galaxy: the Galactic Center.

From above, the Milky Way is a typical spiral galaxy, with sweeping arms which contain stars and nebulae and where most stars are generated. The major arms of our galaxy are named Cygnus, Perseus, Sagittarius, and Centaurus. Our solar system is located roughly halfway—or 25,000 light-years—from the Galactic Center, in the Cygnus arm.

The Milky Way is spinning like a cosmic record, moving through space in the direction of the Virgo Cluster. Our Sun orbits the center of the galaxy with a velocity of roughly 230 kilometers per second, completing a revolution every 250 million years or so. The last time we were in our current galactic position, dinosaurs had yet to walk the Earth.

curs to me that perhaps I underestimate all our motives. Perhaps the main reason we hide our own galactic core is that it is so precious. We are afraid that the moment we expose it we will become vulnerable, like a child. Yet this is exactly why we should try to uncover our galactic heart. To remove all the dust that we have accumulated over time and let our true nature shine.

DR. FIORELLA TERENZI

But there is another aspect to the story of the Hidden Heart. Throughout the ages, virtually every poet, philosopher, and theologian has come to the conclusion that all true and important worldly knowledge begins with self-knowledge: "Know thyself." "To thine own self be true."

At first look, the idea of knowing oneself appears to be relatively simple. After all, one's object of study is *right here*. But then comes the paradoxical realization: It is precisely *because* the Looker and the Looked-At are right here occupying the same space at the same time that the object of study is so very difficult to see. Nearly impossible. The Looker keeps getting in his or her own way.

In physics, there is a phenomenon known as the Heisenberg Uncertainty Principle, which posits that the very act of examining an object changes the physical properties of that object. The simplest example of this principle is found in cases where light is needed to examine the object—the object, of course, reacts to this light, so it is not precisely the same object that it is in total darkness. There is no doubt in my mind that a variation on this principle applies to personal self-examination.

In astrophysics, the problem of knowledge of the galactic core has a similar obstacle: At this historical moment in space technology, we are unable to get far enough away from our own galaxy to get a good look at it. Our solar system is located roughly halfway—about 25,000 light-years—from the center of our galaxy; and the Sun takes about 240 million years to complete one orbit around the center of our galaxy. To get outside our galaxy—in order to look back—we would need a spacecraft able to travel, self-sustained, for thousands of thousands of years, all the while transmitting data back to Earth. But for all our technological progress, we remain far from that capability. So for now, we live in a castle so vast that we can never find our way outside to see how its exterior looks.

In a similar way, it is difficult for humans to acquire self-knowledge: We find it hard to get outside of ourselves to look back and see ourselves and our behavior completely. It seems to me that this analogy to galactic "self-knowledge" extends even further: The "larger" one's personality, the more difficult it is to get outside of oneself for a little self-examination. Someone with a powerful and all-pervasive ego often finds it very difficult to get "beyond" herself to look back. Everywhere she looks, there her effervescent personality is—she can never go beyond its reaches to see her private *self*. When I think about this, I understand why monks say that you must make yourself very small if you are ever to fully understand yourself. A life of monastic withdrawal is one way to pursue that—although it is certainly not something I could ever imagine doing.

But as always, peering through my telescope offers me

a clue to a human puzzle. Astronomy suggests a new technique for gaining self-knowledge: parallel affinity. One way in which astronomers learn about our own galaxy is by peering out at our "twin" galaxy, Andromeda, the biggest and brightest galaxy in our Local Group of galaxies, a mere 2 million light-years away. Though twice the mass of the Milky Way, Andromeda has a similar spiral structure, and so we use Andromeda as a "mirror" to understand our own galaxy.

I have found that this is also a good technique for looking at myself—seeking my "mirror" in other people and studying them for clues to my own character and patterns of behavior, comparing their past experiences with my own, checking how they reacted and what steps they took while passing through particular phases of their lives.

Nova Yourself

The wind picks up, the cloud cover passes. Again the magnificent panoply of the visible Universe reveals itself. I shiver in the damp grass.

In my family, it was said that as a person is at five years old, so shall she be at thirty—and at sixty and ninety. The die is cast in our infancy, and all that remains for us to do is to live out our immutable nature. This is a thought that as a child I never liked or believed—in this way it is true that I have not changed. And from gazing at the sky with the benefit of the galactic histories we astronomers have been able to deduce from our data, I know that such immutability does not even apply to those seemingly most undeviating of all objects, stars.

In 1572, there occurred the most spectacular astronomical event ever witnessed on Earth with the naked eye—a star, Tycho, in the constellation Cassiopeia exploded in a supernova so bright that it outshone every object in the sky, with the exception of the Sun and the full Moon. At its source, it poured out more light than a billion of our Suns; more light, even, than that produced by an entire galaxy of stars. For months, Tycho's light could be seen on our planet even during daylight. On Earth, our 16th Century forebears were astonished—some saw it as a sign of the Endtime, the Second Coming. But for the Danish astronomer who gave the star its name, Tycho Brahe, the event was astounding because a star had appeared where none had been seen before. As he wrote, "When I had satisfied myself that no star of that kind had ever shone forth before, I was led into such perplexity by the unbelievability of the thing that I began to doubt the faith of my own eyes." (Doubting one's eyes was, to be sure, a serious problem for an astronomer in the days before astrophotography.)

The term *nova,* meaning "a new star," turned out, of

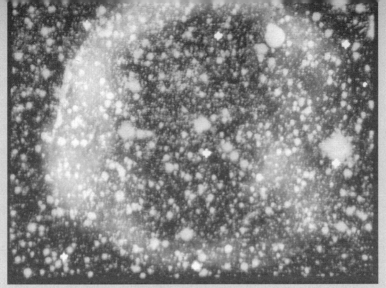

Tycho's Star
NATIONAL OPTICAL ASTRONOMY OBSERVATORIES

TYCHO'S STAR

This faint, almost invisible, wisp of nebula in the constellation Cassiopeia is all that remains of one of the most spectacular astronomical events ever seen from Earth, the supernova *Tycho's Star*.

It is an indication of the enormous force of the supernova explosion that gave rise to this nebula that astronomers have been unable to locate in this image (or any other) an object that can be identified as the exploding star itself.

Far from being mere profligate expenditures of energy, supernovas like Tycho's Star play an essential part in the creation of planetary systems and even life itself. Solar systems and planets like Earth are constructed from heavier elements such as iron and oxygen. These elements are manufactured only in the interiors of stars and would never find their way into planetary systems were they not flung into interstellar space by forces like supernova explosions.

course, to be a misnomer. The star was not new, it had simply become so bright that it had become visible to the unassisted eye for the first time. The later term *supernova* applies to massive stars that explode with a hundred-billionfold increase in luminosity as compared with the mere thousandfold increases of a nova. But by the time the supernova had earned this name, it was known that these stars themselves were not new—it was only the immense thermonuclear explosions that gave them their supervisibility.

It is the origin of this spectacular explosion that again causes me to wonder about the human enigma of how fast to burn—and when. In some cases, the supernova begins when the core of the star reaches the end of its cosmic, billions-of-years life. At the moment of its demise, it collapses on itself under the force of its own gravity, thus liberating an incredible amount of energy that expels the entire mass of the star into the void. Thus, it ends its life in a blaze billions of times brighter and more powerful than it has ever produced before. The moth and the flame again—or so it seems.

But there is more to this story, and it gives me another perspective on the risks and rewards of burning fast and bright—and about the possibilities of change, both cosmic and human.

For other types of supernovas, the end marks the beginning of something truly original. As the star collapses over time, hydrogen atoms become fused, creating helium; and when that helium burns, it creates carbon; the carbon, burning at extraordinarily high temperatures, forms neon, oxygen, and finally silicon, ending with the fusion of the silicon to form iron—a core of iron. And when the iron core collapses under its own gravitational force, the outer layers are expelled in a tremendous explosion to reveal a core of nuclear density—a neutron star.

Voilà, a new core for a new star! The transformation is complete. From an incredibly dramatic death comes a magnificent new star with a life of its own. It is a phenomenon straight out of virtually every cosmology for our time: Out of death comes rebirth.

But not every nova or supernova comes full circle— some simply die in a flame of glory and that is it. That is the risk, the unknowable factor when it comes to choosing to suddenly burn bright and fast, to give it all in one burst.

Lying here, I find myself recalling a day in my terrestrial life when I felt that the end of one of my fondest dreams had come, when a series of seriocomic events made me believe that the Cosmos was conspiring against me and that I should just give up and go back to quietly burning with a low flame.

I had been given an extraordinary opportunity to record my new songs with two powerful producers for A&M Records, a deal that, like so many breaks in my life, had come my way through intense perseverance.

And so I found myself on an airplane, bound from Los Angeles to New York, filled with anticipation. This would be the next big step in my synthesis of music and astrophysics, in acoustically communicating both my astronomical knowledge and my celestial wonder.

Inside the airplane's pressurized cabin, everyone is watching the movie, but I raise the shade a few inches to sneak a look at the sky. Behind me, I can still make out the red-blue line of sunset fading in the west, but here and ahead of us is the inky night sky. Although I know that in a relative sense I am only insignificantly closer to the stars than when I am on the ground, I somehow feel more connected to them up here, hurtling through the atmosphere above my planet like a satellite. For a long, serene moment, I experience that wonderful affinity with the starscape that I first felt as a child, that sense both of oneness with it all and of my infinitely small place in the grand pattern. . . . And then I hear a flight attendant announce that we are landing. I kiss the stars goodbye and prepare to debark.

A limousine is waiting to take me to Carmel, New York, where the recording studio is located. I have reserved a room in a hotel there so that I can wake up the next morning and immediately begin to work.

I am no sooner in the backseat of the limousine than the

driver sneezes. "God bless you," I say, and the driver thanks me, only to sneeze again. And again. And again. I study him in his rearview mirror: His nose is dripping; he is coughing and wheezing—the poor fellow has a terrible cold, perhaps even the flu . . . and I am trapped in here with him for the next two hours! I have only two days of studio time allotted to me in A&M's packed schedule; if I catch this man's cold, that will be it—with my voice gone, this golden opportunity will vanish. I roll down my window and roll up my turtleneck sweater so that it covers my mouth and nose like a surgical mask. I take tiny breaths, as if that will somehow lessen the possibility of infection.

We finally arrive at the hotel, a fabulous-looking edifice in an evergreen grove, and the tragicomedy continues.

I am shown to the last room at the end of an enormous corridor. At last I am alone in my own room; finally I can get the sleep I desperately need to give the performance of my life. I flop onto the king-size bed and close my eyes. And then I hear it—a sound like a coal truck dumping its load down a cellar chute. I raise my head—the sound stops. I return my head to the pillow—the sound resumes, except this time it feels like the dump truck has positioned itself right next to my bed and is discharging its payload directly into my ear. It is an acoustical nightmare!

I dash to the window—not a truck, coal or otherwise, in sight. I open the door to my room and peer into the hallway.

There, crushing away like a stone grinder, is an ice-making machine, producing a new load of cubes every five minutes. I call the front desk. Nothing to be done but put me in another room, they say. I look at my watch—it is three-thirty in the morning, only five and a half hours until I am to appear at the studio, ready to record.

By the time I am ensconced in my new room, unpacked, in my nightgown, and ready to grab a few hours' sleep, I realize that I am shivering. Could I be coming down with the limo driver's cold already? I check the thermometer on the wall—fifty degrees. I turn up the thermostat, take a shower, and return. The temperature has dropped to forty-eight! I call the desk. "Oh yes," they say. "We've been having trouble with the heat in 306. We'll put you in another room."

At six-thirty, I finally close my eyes in a heated room without ice machine accompaniment. At seven-thirty, the phone rings: my wake-up call. I notice that when I say hello my voice is scratchy. Not an auspicious start for a day of vocalizing.

And suddenly, there I am in the soundproof booth of the recording studio across a glass window from the two hottest producers in popular music. I am exhausted, I look like I have been run over by a truck (or an ice machine), and my throat feels like it has become inhabited by a rotary sander. It is time for me to do my thing, to transport these two giants to that point in galactic space where vibrations evoke images of distant stars, where the beat of the pulsars transform into visions of infinite space. Now! Do it now, Fiorella!

Yet all I feel like doing is disappearing. I have never felt so insecure, so unsure of my talent, of my ability to meet my expectations. I have lost all faith in myself. Yes, this is what I am feeling right here in the glass booth with those two expectant faces staring at me. It is no use even trying to make music—I am wasted, depleted, not even my voice is in my control.

But at that moment something quite remarkable happens: I transcend it all! In a fraction of a second, my fear of being myself, for good or for bad, vanishes. I am me, Fiorella, whatever my limitations may be. And that is what I have to offer. Suddenly sound is pouring out of me with a power and lyricism that I have never before possessed, not even after days of preparation, rest, and pampering myself. No sound remotely like this, in fact. And even as I sing, even as I see those faces across from me falling under the spell of this strange, emotion-laden, galactic music, I realize what is happening: I am burning as fast and as brightly as I can with all that is left in me. I am giving all!

And I am risking everything I have, too. Because I realize that this one supreme effort could in the end leave me with nothing left over. Like my friends and colleagues who experienced one brief moment of brilliance that exhausted them, like a meteorite that suddenly bursts into a white flame and then dies, burned out.

But it keeps pouring out of me with the same intensity, the same ethereal lyricism. And when I begin the next composition, it comes out even more strongly, more melodiously. I hear myself creating as I go along, improvising harmonies and countermelodies that have never before occurred to me. And it is then, listening to myself, that I realize that what has happened is that I have become something new. Exhausted and depleted like a dying star, the old me—all my insecurities—has burned out with a luminosity a billion times more intense than ever before, but now, in its place, is a new core around which my new life is only beginning.

As both a scientist and an artist, I must confront the truth—always a daunting task, especially when it means facing my own limits and imperfections. Behind the microphone on that particular day, I was faced with every one of them. Here were all my limitations right in front of me, all the terrifying thoughts I had so successfully avoided for so long. I had to face them all if I wanted to go on—and in that explosive confrontation there was a personal miracle: *My imperfections became my best qualities! My insecurities became that special expression in my voice that made my singing style*

unique! My fear of performing erupted into my passion for music.
I was finally expressing who I really was. I was nova-ing myself!

No Momma, no Poppa, we are not set in stone at the age of five. Not if we work hard and fearlessly, not if we are determined and willing to change, not if we pick the right time to explode—to take the risk of transforming ourselves by giving everything we have. Some of us dare to supernova!

Lost Souls, White Dwarves, Being, and Nothingness

The sky abruptly inverts. Where just a moment ago I saw stars, I now see the empty spaces between them. It is like the experience of gazing at that gestalt drawing that suddenly transforms from a vase to two facing profiles in silhouette.

I am lost in space, overcome by a wave of melancholy. I know that in some of these spaces stars once existed—stars that have undergone gravitational collapse, that have shrunk down and can no longer generate energy. White dwarves, they are called—a fittingly gloomy name. These white dwarves have turned so completely in on themselves that they no longer give off light. They cannot shine.

For centuries, we mortals believed that stars were immortal—but, of course, they are not. Stars die in different

WHITE DWARF

A *white dwarf* is a very-small-radius star that has used up all the fuel in its interior. This dying star has a very faint brightness. Having exhausted all its thermonuclear fuel, it is destined to collapse on itself under its own gravity, contracting down to a high-density sphere roughly the same size as the Earth. Because of their very low luminosity, white dwarves are very difficult to detect.

ways, and the nature of a star's fate depends in large part on its mass. Stars that are less than four times the mass of our Sun never develop the necessary central pressures or temperatures to ignite thermonuclear reactions that use carbon or oxygen as a fuel. During their final spasms, these dying stars eject up to 60 percent of their matter. The stellar core cools down with a sharp inward turn, contracting until the stars become what are called white dwarves.

There is no turning back at this stage, no last-chance possibility to suddenly ignite additional fuels inside the heart of these dying stars, so the crushing weight of their gases presses in from all sides, compressing the stellar corpse. Contracted down to a sphere roughly the size of the Earth, these stellar corpses have a high density, but they have lost their visibility—they are too small and faint to be seen with the naked eye. They are lost forever in interstellar space. . . .

Gina lived next door to me in Milan. She was a lovely, delicate woman with four cats. For years, she was totally devoted to one man, and during this time she shone with such an aura of happiness that everyone around her reflected her joy. . . .

But then Gina's man suddenly left her for a younger woman, and Gina immediately began a strange phase in her life, a long unwavering withdrawal into herself. She seemed to physically shrink before our eyes: Her shoulders slumped, her eyes grew dim; she turned so completely in on herself that she was literally disappearing. . . .

Like a dying white dwarf, she started to close in on herself, barely living as she gradually used up her inner fuel. No encouragement from the outside world seemed to help her. I tried to get her to go out with me, to meet people.

"You do not have to fall in love again," I told her. "But neither do you have to forsake everything and everyone in your life because of your loss."

But Gina would not budge; she wanted to be left alone. She seemed to have reached a point from which there was no turning back. She had totally turned in on herself. She not only despaired of ever finding another man to love, but she felt also that she had lost the necessary emotional energy to start over again even if she did find someone.

All that marvelous energy that had once illuminated her life and shone upon her friends was now channeled to her core, where she burned invisibly into nonexistence. . . .

When I learned that she had taken her own life, I was deeply saddened. I racked my brain and heart—was there anything I could have done to save her?

I stare into the void, meditating on all the lost souls who have turned away from the Universe around them and collapsed upon themselves, collapsed into oblivion. . . .

Prime-Time Starcast

Living in Los Angeles, I frequently come into contact with people who are anxiously concerned about their "permanence." Will their television series be renewed? Will anyone remember their last record? Will their film still be talked about next year? Five years from now? A hundred?

I have seen friends drive themselves crazy with worry over such questions. They desperately want their lives to have some kind of lasting impact—or, at the very least, an impact that lasts for the entire television season. I am pretty sure that when the word *star* evolved to its present, euphemistic, show business meaning, it was meant to capture stellar "permanence" just as much as stellar "brightness."

"You are lucky," one of my Hollywood friends once said to me. "You get to work with everlasting things while I live in a world of 'Here today, gone tomorrow.' "

"Not exactly," I replied. I explained to him that in the grand scheme of the Universe, even stars are impermanent. I told him about the sad fate of the white dwarf, how its interior eventually crystallizes to a carbon-oxygen diamond so cold that all molecular motion stops.

"Even our own Sun will eventually end up that way," I told him.

This, of course, did not cheer up my friend at all—not that it was exactly meant to. I simply wanted to give him a little perspective on the relative "permanence" of things Out There. I decided to tell him a little about the most relative of all galactic phenomena, time.

"Every object you see is in the past because it takes time for the light reflecting off an object to reach your eyes," I began. "It goes fast—186,000 miles per second—but it still takes time. It takes only the tiniest fraction of a second to travel from my face to your eye, but nonetheless it *is* the past of my face that you are seeing."

I went on to explain that elapsed time from object to eye gets more impressive when you look up at the Sun. That life-supporting star is 93 million miles away, so our perception of it is always eight minutes old. If the fires of the Sun were suddenly extinguished, we would not know about it for eight minutes.

As an astronomer, I am constantly peering into the past. At times, I will spend several earthly hours examining a celestial object that actually ceased to exist a million or more years ago! No, my friend, I do not exactly work with the everlasting.

The idea that I am actually looking at the distant past still dazzles me as much as the first time I fully understood what it meant to say "Distance equals time"—that the farther away one looks in the Universe, the farther back in time one is seeing. I told my friend about a recent night at the observatory when I was gazing at Abell 1367, one of the richest known clusters of galaxies, which is located in the constellation Leo, approximately 400 million light-years away. A light-year is the distance light travels in a year, so the Abell 1367 I was viewing was 400 million years old! I was looking directly at the past. I was observing what had existed 400 million years ago!

But then, I wondered, what exactly is this "present time" in which I exist?

It was two in the morning, and I was alone with the stars, the kind of setup that gets my imagination spinning wildly. And I had this thought: What if there were a giant mirror strung between those stars? And what if that mirror reflected light back across those 400 million light-years to

Planet Earth? Could I then behold an image of Earth that was almost a billion years old? Would I be peering into our own prehistoric past, deep into the Precambrian Era?

I would not see myself in this reflection. Nor would I see the observatory, telescope, or buildings of any kind. Not a single sign of life. Just a bare outcropping of rock. If I were on Abell 1367 now, I would be looking back at my home planet as it was 400 million years ago!

Fantasy or not, I know that this potential image of the past of my planet exists somewhere in the Universe! And this idea imbues the present—my "now"—with an almost-dreamlike quality.

"Doesn't the idea of 'permanence' feel kind of arbitrary when you think about things like that?" I said to my anxious Hollywood friend.

He nodded soberly and was silent for a moment. But then he looked at me and said, "But wouldn't it be nice if 400 million years from now somebody could look back in time at our planet and see my TV series?"

A Star by Any Other Name

A long time has passed since my ancestors named the heavenly bodies after the human and godlike characteristics they seemed to embody. Mars, Venus, Mercury, Orion . . . At this moment, I wish these ancient stargazers were still around, assigning names to what they see, instead of the current crop of name givers—the scientists who are more in love with numbers than with poetry.

Names shape the way we perceive things. If instead of naming me Fiorella (Little Flower), my parents had chosen to name me Lupa (Wolf), people around me might have seen me as a different kind of person—perhaps as a more cunning and aggressive little girl than a Fiorella.

This is certainly true about heavenly bodies. Mars by any other name would probably not be perceived by the average stargazer as a potential fortress of bizarre-looking creatures intent on invading Planet Earth. It all began with that name of the Roman god of war. Incidentally, I am not surprised that so many people believe in extraterrestrial abductions by Martians. I take this phenomenon as a sign of a *mass yearning* very much like the kind experienced by ancients and primitives who deeply felt the desolation of being isolated in a Universe they did not understand. Believing in extraterrestrials, no matter how belligerent they are thought to be, means believing that we are not alone.

In a similar way we see the highly visible, brightly glowing Planet Venus as soft and feminine; the many-mooned Jupiter as magisterial; and the rapidly orbiting Mercury as conscientious. The grouping of stars we call the Big Dipper, with its allusion to an elegantly simple water ladle, gives rise to feelings of hearth and home in the country, while the more recently named black hole, describing collapsed stars whose surface gravity is so strong that not even light can escape, calls to mind some kind of cosmic existential dread, the ultimate "No Exit."

All of these names make cosmic objects somehow more accessible and comprehensible. Give a heavenly object a name that is a metaphor for something in terrestrial culture and you make it your own. It allows us to build a personal cosmology peopled with planets and stars, galaxies and black holes, all with human and human-goddess/god characteristics that are familiar to us.

But somehow the celestial catalog ended up as a mishmash of terminology. I could understand it if astronomers eschewed personal, evocative names for heavenly objects in favor of a single, unified system for classifying them. But instead we came up with an arbitrary, confusing, and difficult-to-remember system of names for heavenly bodies. Planets are named after Roman gods; the moons of Mars and Jupiter have Greek names, although Uranus's moons are named after characters in Shakespeare's plays, with one little moon named Puck.

And then things really start to get confusing. Bright stars come bearing a mix of Arabic, Greek, and Latin names, while medium-bright stars are designated by a mix of Greek letters combined with their constellation's Latin genitive form, as in Alpha Centauri. Fainter stars get a number plus the Latin addition, like 51 Pegasi. And the faintest stars get a combination of letters and numbers without benefit of a constellation designation, as in the euphonious HDE 226868. Only a few dozen galaxies have genuine names like Andromeda (named after the mythological Ethiopian princess who was fastened to a rock for a sea monster to devour but was saved by Perseus.)

Asteroids are not very lucky, either. They are named with a number that corresponds to their year of discovery. Comets are no better off; they are often named after their discoverers, such as Halley's Comet or Shoemaker-Levy 9. Novas and supernovas also take their names from their year of discovery.

I long for celestial names that have more personal relevance, names that give me images and stories to connect with. An object called HDE 226868 brings nothing human to mind. It does not help me feel related to the Universe the way the names Venus and Mercury do. A name like HDE 226868 numbs my imagination—it gives me nothing to fantasize about, to attach properties to. It offers no fanciful way to even remember it. HDE 226868 reduces the object it stands for to the level of an item in a hardware catalog. Science has been much more respectful in naming plants and insects than in naming heavenly bodies.

I believe that if there had been more women astronomers we would probably find ourselves with a more poetic stellar nomenclature today. Men tend to find comfort in numeration; women are more likely to find it in fantasy and imagination. I realize, of course, that there are far too many items out there in the Cosmos for us to dub them all with interesting, humanly relevant names. We cannot, like Adam and Eve, set out to give a name to every one of God's heavenly creations. But should we not at least try to give a meaningful name to every heavenly body that we encounter in the sky?

Some people will probably say, "There she goes again, trying to turn astronomy into some kind of fairy tale." But actually I believe the opposite is true—by giving objects names, we make them real. And if these names are personally meaningful instead of cold and calculated, we demystify the objects. We take them out of the realm of the irrelevant and make Them and Us parts of the Same Thing. That is not a fairy tale, we *are* parts of the Same Thing—the Universe.

And so I want to give a humanly relevant name to the pair Quasar 0351+206 in the constellation Taurus, deeply embedded in its neighboring galaxy. These two quasars are tangentially paired, yet 0351+206 radiates so much energy that it all but obliterates the view of its neighbor with its intense emissions. I yearn for a name that captures this relationship! I yearn for a name that instantly brings to mind Quasar 0351+206's color and brilliance, its dominance and self-effacing charm. And so I rename this quasar Evita!

And what about that asteroid orbiting between Mars and Jupiter that is known as 4331? It is such a tiny planetoid and so devoid of distinguishing features that my first thought is that maybe it does not deserve a more captivating name. Yet there is something so steady and earnest about the way it goes about its business of orbiting the Sun just as faithfully as the major planets do. It goes on and on, plugging away, chugging away, never losing sight of its mission. Yes, that's it; this little asteroid reminds me of that children's inspirational story, "The Little Engine That Could," and so that shall be its name. No more 4331; henceforth, Little Engine. Perhaps with this name the little asteroid will inspire me to be steadier and more earnest each time I view it.

I lie here on the Italian hillside christening the human star population. It is as if I have just inherited thousands of children in need of names. And with the names I give them, their distinct personalities come alive.

I feel peaceful and full of optimism. I am creating a sky full of companions. With these names, these heavenly bodies become part of a human cosmology, a place where we can wander among familiar friends.

DR. FIORELLA TERENZI

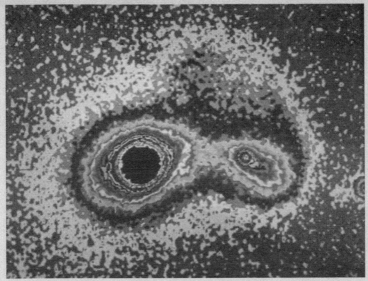

Quasar 0351 + 206

QUASAR 0351 + 206

Quasars originally got their name for being "quasi-stellar" in nature, since they were points in the sky like stars but did not share the typical spectra seen in stars. It is now believed that they are extremely distant galaxies—farther away than most normal galaxies that have been observed.

Quasars can be seen because of a powerful engine that lives in the heart of the galaxy. These engines are believed to be massive black holes whose surrounding accretion disks produce more energy than the entire galaxies in which they reside.

Salve Carissimo, *Asteroid Felix, sleek and stealthy as a cat. Hey, Pale Star Sophia, once so luminously beautiful, now fading so gracefully. Hello, Meteor Sylvester, so flashy yet so ephemeral. . . .*

And a kiss to you out there, my dearest friend, my invisible collaborator in sublime music, Galaxy Giuseppe Verdi.

COSMIC CANVAS

"Life imitates art and art imitates science."

I stand transfixed in front of van Gogh's Starry Night, *the Dutch painter's legendary depiction of Saint-Remy-de-Provence at night. At first look, the painting is quite disturbing—those swirling stars evoke a dizzy sense of chaos. But as I continue to gaze at the painting, a feeling of stillness and tranquility flows into me. . . .*

I recently read of an enterprising art historian at UCLA, Alan Boime, who compared the stellar array in *Starry Night* with a Griffith Observatory reconstruction of that predawn sky in Saint-Remy on the night of June 19, 1889; he found that van Gogh had been perfectly faithful to what he saw. What is more, Boime discovered that van Gogh had a genuine interest in astronomy through the writings of the French astronomer Camille Flammarion. And so the popular idea that the hallucinogenic style of this painting represents van Gogh's madness appears not to be the whole truth. On the contrary, it seems that under the influence of Flammarion's analyses of planetary and stellar systems, van Gogh was trying to evoke the themes of universal harmony, eternity, and immortality.

That is certainly the ultimate effect the painting has on me.

What inspires awe inspires art—the elegant curves of a beautiful woman's figure, the stark planes of a Roman ruin in an Arcadian landscape, the relentless tides of the ocean, the heavenly bodies that traverse the sky. Art and artifacts from ancient Egypt to the present day record and celebrate that most awe-inspiring of phenomena, the Cosmos. There is something so soul-stirring about staring out into the Universe, something so inherently aesthetic in the Earth's-eye view of this jewel-studded overhead vault, that painters, poets, sculptors, architects, and musicians have always been inspired to make art from their vision of it. In friezes and medallions, in frescoes and paintings, in church domes and spiral ramps, in poems and symphonies, the world of astronomy is rendered in human proportions and in a human vocabulary. These artists at once hallow the heavens and make them relevant to our earthly lives.

Celestial Architecture

Several summers ago, I was invited to be the guest of a colleague, Professor Roberto Caruso, at his home in Agrigento, Sicily. I had a writing project to complete—a chapter on radioactivity for the University of Milan's textbook on Terrestrial Physics—and a villa on the Mediterranean seemed like a perfect spot to get it done. No clubs or concerts or phone calls to tempt me away from my work. Just my computer and me . . . and my deadline.

What I had not taken into account, of course, was the biggest distraction of them all: the overwhelmingly beautiful Sicilian landscape. Just the blue of the Mediterranean is enough to lift me out of my skin for an azure-colored Time Travel. . . .

I tell myself, "Only a quick break on the terrace and then I will go back to work. Back to the data on radiocarbon dating, back to the nuclei and particles. Just a breath of sea air and it's back to business again. . . ."

I pull open the thick blue curtain that serves as the front door and I am greeted by the brilliant light of the Mediterranean sky. What a contrast! Going from the cool darkness of my room and my tiny computer screen to this bright, limitless vista! I feel as if I have just escaped from Plato's cave and a different reality is now in front of my eyes. . . .

I seat myself on a brightly painted chair, already feeling the heat of the Sun on my shoulders and arms. Inside, I can hear Professor Caruso pounding away industriously on his computer.

"I'll be back in a moment," I mouth silently. "Just giving my mind a little rest. . . ."

Everywhere I look, I see patterns of blue and white—blue sky, white clouds; blue sea, white sand; blue shutters, white walls. The sea breeze wafts up to me, caressing my skin. The sea is so still I cannot see where the water ends and the sky begins. . . .

The Sun is like a spotlight, picking out the very center of this landscape with its brightest rays. And there it shines, that earthly glimmer of Eternity, the Valle dei Templi and its Greek temples from the 5th Century B.C. *Over there the Temple Giove, and there the Temple Giunone, and over there the Temple della Concordia with its thirty-four limestone columns weathered to the color of gold by millennia of sunlight. From here, they look like portals to another time—a time when our environment was very different, but the sky was virtually the same. . . .*

My mind wanders further afield, and I see another ancient structure. This one is composed of four concentric circles of mammoth sandstones. It is Stonehenge, on the Salisbury Plain in southern England.

Radiocarbon-dated at from 3000 to 2500 B.C., Stonehenge is the oldest known astronomical observatory still standing. Its original thirty stones included fifty- and sixty-ton uprights that supported massive lintels in a circle almost

Stonehenge, Salisbury Plain, England
E.C. KRUPP, GRIFFITH OBSERVATORY

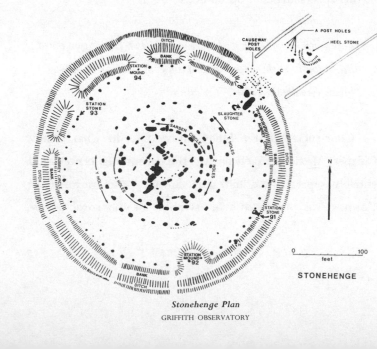

Stonehenge Plan
GRIFFITH OBSERVATORY

a hundred feet in diameter. These appear to have been erected to align with key seasonal positions of the Sun. Perhaps these very early astronomers hoped to predict eclipses (a phenomenon that has always frightened and fascinated people). But what is most striking about this hilltop structure is its haunting beauty. For me, it has the feeling of a primordial cathedral—stark and elegant, austere and inspiring. It reflected the dance of heavenly bodies in a stunning man-made object. In order to understand the splendor and symmetry Out There, humankind echoed it Down Here and in the process created a magnificent piece of architecture.

Of course, at the time it was constructed, Stonehenge was both observatory *and* temple, laboratory *and* altar. Science, religion, and aesthetics were all One Thing, deeply influenced by the spectacle of the sky. And they were united in this spectacular hilltop edifice.

Again, the image changes before my eyes. I know it is not Agrigento; it is the deep, thick jungle of Mexico. I see the Mayan ceremonial center, Yaxchilán.

Constructed in the 5th Century B.C. in what is now Chiapas, Mexico, Yaxchilán was the ceremonial center of an entirely separate and different culture—the Maya. Their Cosmos was populated with symbols of the royal family, the Bird Jaguars, as well as a variety of other mythological figures, including some terrifying monsters. The images on Yaxchilán's carved stone stelae and lintels, as well as the spatial arrangement of its various temples, served as a paradigm of the right way to live in relation to their Sacred Cosmos. It was as if the language of the Cosmos had been rendered in stone.

But again, it is the beauty of the place that gets to me. And again this eerie, exotic architectural wonder was inspired by astronomical calculations. . . .

One image slides away, replaced by another. In front of me on the same hill I now see that incredible masterpiece of 12th Century Khmer architecture, the Hindu temple Angkor Wat, in Cambodia, Southeast Asia.

Some theories based on recent measurements of this temple and its grounds suggest that the entire pattern of the place may have been based on numbers derived from both the solar and lunar calendars of that day. For example, the axes and circumference of its outermost enclosure appear to record the solar and lunar years, while the second gallery records numbers related to the Moon. The entire setup is aligned with solar and lunar orbits—sighting lines extend from Angkor Wat's long western causeway to its central towers. Once again, I am gazing at heavenly architecture

Yaxchilán, Chiapas, Mexico
E.C. KRUPP, GRIFFITH OBSERVATORY

Angkor Wat, Cambodia
E.C. KRUPP, GRIFFITH OBSERVATORY

inspired by cosmic patterns—stellar art inspired by stellar observations.

Perhaps the pleasing proportions of this Hindu temple can be attributed to the harmonious proportions of the celestial movements they symbolize? The celestial bodies inspired the mathematicians to calculate their movements. . . . Their calculations might have inspired the artists who designed the temple. . . . The temple might have inspired the faithful to open their hearts to the wonders of the Universe.

This circle of Cosmic Inspiration revolves before my eyes . . . and suddenly I am back on my brightly painted chair in Agrigento. From the corner of my eye, I see that Professor Caruso has stepped out onto the terrace. I observe him. He appears to be on a time journey of his own. Ah, even this revered professor is a man who can still daydream, a man who is still transported by beauty. I immediately feel a new kinship with Professor Caruso, and I know this connection will change the way we relate to each other from now on.

I smile at him and say, "I guess we should probably go back in."

He smiles back and we duck through the blue curtain to return to work. Wistfully I return to the darkened room where I write. Back to particles and nuclei. . . .

But, yes, these are awe-inspiring, too.

Cosmic Art

For once, I wish I were in an Italian train station instead of an American one. In Italy, the trains are *dependably* late— you know you can sit down for a leisurely gelato in the station café at the precise moment when your train is supposed to leave. But in New York, they leave right on time, so I will have to tear myself away from gazing at the ceiling of Grand Central Terminal.

What a wonder it is! A Grand Celestial Vault arching over a cavernous waiting room that is filled with people rushing from one earthly destination to another. This ceiling depicts the constellations with pin-lights as stars and connect-the-dot line drawings of Orion and Cassiopeia and all the others. Looking up at it, I feel the grandeur of the sky, but I also feel as if the stars are almost within my reach. What a tantalizing thought. This silent, fixed, eternal sky looms over us train-catching mortals as we rush from point A to point B on the Earth's surface. It reminds us of the relative brevity of our own journeys—and of Life's journey. That is exactly what good art can do: remind us of these cosmic truths.

But now the light is flashing at the gate to my train, so I, too, must rush on my way from point A to point B. My destination is upstate New York, where I will be spending a weekend in the country with my friend Tina, a painter who is devoted to interpreting celestial themes on her canvases. For her, the shapes and movements of heavenly bodies testify to a Universal Harmony, a harmony that is echoed in human love.

Tina is waiting for me at the small country station. She leads me to a station wagon crammed with paint tubes and brushes and rolls of canvas. The moment we set off for her cabin, she begins to talk excitedly about her recent forays into the art library of a nearby university.

"I was looking at stuff from the Renaissance—this very moody art by Dürer—and the astronomical details turn out to be incredibly sophisticated. Like this Dürer engraving called *Melencolia*—when you look in the background, you can see the trace of a comet as clear as if it had been photographed. I'm sure it is there to emphasize how fast it all goes, both our moods *and* our lives."

"Comet imagery goes back even further than that," I reply, and tell Tina about the Giotto fresco I once saw on the walls of Scrovegni Chapel in Padua; it featured a fuzzy "star" with an unusual detail—a tail. "Several centuries later that fuzzy 'star' was identified as Halley's Comet."

Tina laughed.

"But listen to my latest discovery," she said. "This incredible panel from a Renaissance altarpiece by a painter named Mathias Grünewald. It's called *Christ's Halo,* and believe it or not, it shows this rare type of corona caused by the refraction of sunlight by ice crystals in the upper atmosphere. How's that for astronomical esoterica?''

"It's wonderful," I say. "A perfect symbol for a miracle—a scientific miracle, of course!''

It is only with Tina that I can have conversations like this. Most of my astronomer friends would find this kind of talk too whimsical, and most of my artist friends would find it too technical. But, each in her own way, Tina and I are eternally fascinated by the way art always seems to move parallel to science, especially astronomical art and astronomical science.

As the station wagon pulls onto the dirt road that leads to Tina's cabin, we both fall silent. We are looking out the car window at the beautiful autumn landscape. Sunlight plays through a canopy of multicolored leaves, dappling the leaf-covered ground. I feel as if we are entering a terrestrial Cosmic Canvas. . . .

The Lyrical Sky

We do not have to look further than the lyrics of popular songs to find astronomic allusions in poetry. I could probably fill an entire notebook with just those I know in Italian and English. In lyrics from the forties and fifties, lovers (and unrequited lovers) are forever being bewitched by the Moon, humbled by the number of stars in the sky, wishing on shooting stars, and comparing their love affairs to the transitory flight of a comet. Looking over these lyrics, I sometimes think that the writers of these popular songs believed that lovers spent more time gazing at the sky than into each other's eyes. Who knows? Maybe it is more restful.

But my favorite pop astro-lyrics are from the sixties and seventies and beyond, after the Space Age created an entirely new perspective on the Cosmos. In one Pink Floyd song, the look in a lover's eyes is compared to black holes. How is that for an artist's finding inspiration in the latest astronomic discovery?

And one Rolling Stones song makes a reference to the fiery orange giant star Aldebaran. I love this allusion. Although it is one of the twenty brightest stars in the sky, few people would have ever heard its name if Mick Jagger had not celebrated it in his lyric. I like to think that Mick was simply carrying on in the tradition of Giotto and Dürer: educating the general public about astronomy through his art.

Finally, there is the pure music of the Cosmos, the astronomy-inspired art form that speaks most intimately to me for obvious reasons. Here again, the catalog overflows with examples, ranging from the baroque composer Georg Friedrick Handel's moving aria "Total Eclipse" to the modernist composer Paul Hindemith's dissonant take on the harmony of the spheres, *The Harmony of the World*; and from the cool jazz sounds of Wayne Shorter's "Supernova" to Sun Ra's "Cosmos."

But my favorite of all the astro-music is the popular orchestral suite *The Planets,* by the English composer Gustav Holst. An avid student of both astronomy and astrological mythology, Holst evokes both a telescopic viewing of the seven planets known in his time (early 20th Century) and the mythological gods they symbolize. "Mars, Bringer of War," a drum-and-gong-filled martial piece, launches the suite. Then comes "Venus, Bringer of Peace," invoking utter tranquility. Then the speedy "Mercury, the Winged Messenger" and the sprightly "Jupiter, Bringer of Jollity." Next is the haunting "Saturn, Bringer of Old Age" and the chameleonlike "Uranus, the Magician." Finally, the suite closes with the delicate, lingering "Neptune, the Mystic."

This is music that always pleases a symphony audience, but I save my Bernstein recording of it for a special occasion, one that all-too-few people are privileged to enjoy:

It is almost five in the morning as I finish my telescopic observations for the night. It has been a productive evening, much data collected and stored for future analysis. But there is still almost an hour until dawn, when my scheduled time at the observatory ends.

Quickly, I pull my CD player from my bag and put on

the headphones. Then I set the machinery in motion that aims the telescope at coppery-red Mars. I press "Play," and Gustav Holst's evocative music begins, accompanying me on a pre-dawn journey to The Planets.

THE DNA OF ASTRONOMY

"The Universe celebrates diversity,
whereas human beings tend to suppress it."

Ancient Starscape

Hundreds of thousands of years ago on this Sun-orbiting mass of organic matter, we *Homo sapiens* made our appearance. Everything in front of our eyes was old but also new, not yet seen through the eyes of human interpretation. . . .

Again, darkness descends. I will wait in this, my cave by the river, for the light to reappear. And it will reappear—it always does. But my mind is not at rest. I can hear the crickets outside, the wind shaking the leaves of the trees, the pounding of the river as it rushes by.

Impulsively, I grab a rock and hurl it against the cave wall. A sudden streak of light where it strikes! Incredible! It is like those streaky flashes that I see in the ceiling that curves above me outside of this cave. Are they the same? Is there a larger cave Out There like mine Down Here?

I step out into the night. The river is flooding over its banks again. There seems to be a pattern to this flooding, too, just like the regular alternation of light and darkness. What is it? What controls it?

And what are those twinkling dots scattered across this over-head arch, those bright specks that come and go with the darkness? They at once dazzle and comfort me.

In the evening glow, I take a piece of bone and mark it with dots to match the spectacle that I see above me—an image that I can carry with me while the spectacle itself comes and goes. And while fashioning this image, I have a perplex-ing realization—whenever that one large, bright, moving dot appears overhead, the river Down Here floods.

How can this be? Why do these two phenomena match? Does it mean that those luminous dots and these raging wa-ters are part of the Same Thing? And if so, am I part of that Same Thing, too?

Does the luminous dot know me? Does it control me in the same way that it controls the flooding of the river?

Out There and Down Here

Since prehistory, the study of the sky has stimulated two lines of human inquiry: the search for regular patterns of nature, particularly those that have utilitarian consequences for the problems of daily life; and the search for a literally "Higher" Power that invests life Down Here with some kind of transcendental meaning.

From the first inquiry came a host of practical solutions to the problems of living. In ancient Egypt, the flooding of the Nile was a substantial problem for farmers, riverside dwellers, and sailors alike. So when the Egyptians observed that this annual flood always occurred as soon as the star Sirius became visible on the eastern horizon, life along the Nile was forever changed. With regularity came predictability; and with predictability came human plans and contingencies. *Now* is a good time to plant—not *then*, because the flood will wash the seeds away. *Now* is a good time to sail—not *then*, because the tide will run your ship aground. The practical consequences of these observations were so important to the people and the economy of ancient Egypt that the most respected and educated members of society— the priests—were charged with this work.

As the people in charge of astronomical observations, the priests acquired considerable power, slowly taking control over the population's daily routines. They not only determined when to plant and when to harvest, and when and where to sail, but when holy days were to be celebrated. Thus, practical advice and ceremonial advice came from one and the same source. United in the pursuit of astronomy, science and religion were linked together like binary stars. Centuries would pass before they would set off on separate courses.

The spiritual component of stargazing derived from more than just the authority of the priests; it came from ordinary people's observations. As well as finding a regularity to live by in the skies, people found thunder, hurricanes, meteor showers, comets—scary stuff. The heavens contained order *and* disorder; they engendered security *and* fear. In this duality we can see the beginnings of the immutable *and* capricious, comforting *and* punishing Old Testament God.

People also understood that practical solutions are not meanings. Flood warnings may make their lives much easier, but these warnings do not in themselves imbue their lives with purpose. Calendars and maps may give people tools for plotting the comings and goings of their daily lives, but they do not tell them *why* they are here, *what* is important, or *what it means* to lead a significant life.

So Man and Woman also looked to the awe-inspiring spectacle of the sky to answer these basic philosophical questions of meaning and purpose. After all, if we see that the Moon and stars control our tides, it is not a cosmic leap to believe that these and other heavenly bodies also have a profound influence on other parts of our lives—including our souls.

DR. FIORELLA TERENZI

Stellar Culture

One of the prime tasks of anthropology is to uncover the common denominators of cultures that have developed independently of one another. Did both the Aztecs and the Chinese develop arithmetic? Did both the Navajos and the ancient Greeks have a category for past events? Did all cultures develop music on their own?

The answers to questions like these provide us with what anthropologists call "cultural universals"—those elements and characteristics that simply grow out of the fact that we are all Human Beings who inhabit Planet Earth, regardless of exactly where on this planet we make our home, what language we speak, or in which epoch we live.

Heavenly bodies provide the basis for many of these cultural universals. Wherever on Earth Man and Woman have been, they have looked up at the heavens, by day and by night, and seen something Out There that is connected to life Down Here—gods, geometry, art and architectural forms, mythology and folklore, mathematics and philosophy, synchrony and harmony . . .

But do some of these universal inspirations actually come from observing the sky? Or does looking at the sky simply confirm inspirations that already exist within us? Perhaps, I sometimes think, there is a DNA of astronomy. . . .

Our Cosmic Address

One fundamental way in which cultures have always established human meaning is through establishing our Cosmic Address: Where We Are *tells* Who We Are.

The ancient Babylonians figured that Where We Lived was pretty much the totality of the Universe; our world was all there was. The world was thought to be a huge hollow ellipse with oceans above as its shell, and sky and ground in its heart. These ancients had nothing to go on except what they saw with *their* naked eyes from *their* hilltops, just as this was all I had to go on as an untutored child peering out from my grandmother's field.

The Babylonians accounted for their observations with what was for them a logical cosmological setup: Rain was ocean water that trickled down through holes in the solid sky and springs were water squirting up through holes in the solid platform that separated us from the nether ocean. As for those luminous objects that moved across the overhead dome—the Sun and the Moon, stars and planets—they came and went like actors passing through curtained portals in the east and west of the overhead stage. For the casual stargazer living in ancient Babylonia, this elliptical shape, these solid boundaries, and this central position of the world was taken as an article of faith.

The Egyptians believed that the Universe resembled a

rectangular box with the Earth at the bottom and the sky stretched above it. Since the Nile was the only water in the middle of the desert, it figured prominently in their cosmology—it was described as a branch of a vast river that flowed all around the Earth. Sailing on a boat in this river was the living god, Ra, who carried a disk of fire—the Sun—on its course. Ra had to die every night to bring on the darkness, but was reborn every morning.

We are usually taught in school that civilization gradually wended its way toward a scientific cosmology as a result of incremental discoveries in mathematics and technology—the invention of the telescope supplying one of the biggest forward pushes of them all. But cosmology has evolved in fits and starts since the age of the ancients. At times it came close to a purely scientific model of the Universe, but then it backed away from that model for centuries at a time. And when we take a close look at what caused the fits and what caused the starts, we find that major mathematical and technological discoveries tell us only half the story; the other half is told by the psychological, social, and spiritual temperament of the culture. The Egyptians could feel snug and secure because the Nile was so regular in its flooding. On the other hand, the Tigris and Euphrates were wildly unpredictable, and this is, in part, why the Babylonians turned to astrology to try to get help from something more obviously regular. Sometimes I feel that I can take the cultural pulse of a particular time and place in history simply by looking at what twist or turn astronomy took at that specific point in time.

What does a geocentric cosmology tell us about a culture? Or a heliocentric cosmology? How about a cosmology in which everything is in constant motion, as compared with one in which bodies Out There move while Down Here we remain stationary? If we permit ourselves to look at contemporary astrophysics with an anthropologist's eye, what do we learn about a culture from a cosmology that introduces the mind-blowing concept of black holes—those stellar prisons from which not even light can escape? Does our cultural acceptance of black holes imply that ours is a brave and stoic culture? That we live in an Age of Fatalism and Hopelessness? Or does it only mean that we live in a culture that honors the discoveries of serious scientists?

Harmonizing with Pythagoras

The ancient cosmologist with whom I feel the greatest affinity is Pythagoras, the 6th Century B.C. Greek astronomer who introduced the world to the concept of the Harmony of the Spheres. In his time, there was no distinction between philosophy and astronomy—all knowledge was interconnected. One of Pythagoras's major contributions was to suggest that the basis of this interconnectedness was found in numbers.

Numbers not only expressed the relationships among various natural phenomena, they expressed the *cause* of them all. Numbers allowed us to chart the regularities of Nature, the rising and setting of the Sun, and the movement of the stars. Pythagoras was the first to propose a celestial model based *solely* on the movements of heavenly bodies. His insistence on careful observations of celestial bodies and their motions was a momentous shift in the direction of rationalism as the proper way to understand the Universe.

What I find particularly appealing about Pythagoras is the way in which he linked astronomy to music in a cosmic embrace. "Philosophy is the highest music," the astrophysicist/musician philosopher is reputed to have said. I absolutely adore the implications of that statement—it still resonates for this astrophysicist/musician some twenty-five centuries later.

Dear Pythagoras,

Music was so important to you that tones and harmony had to figure in your cosmology, too. Your theory of the Music of the Spheres has in its simplicity a great elegance. It must have almost religious overtones for you.

I concur when you say that music has the potential to produce an ecstatic out-of-body experience transporting hu-

mankind to the realm of that ultimate abstraction—numbers. For you, music leads to numbers—the most "disembodied" entities in the Universe. For you, numbers were both the source of music and its destination.

You discovered the physics of pitch—that the pitch of a note is directly related to the length of the string that produces it—and that tonal intervals follow simple ratios (2:1, an octave; 3:2, a fifth; and so on).

In the same way, by applying numbers to what you saw in the sky, you and your students were able to find some sort of predictable order in the Universe; the musical interval between the Earth and the Moon was a whole tone, between the Moon and Mercury a semitone, between the Sun and Venus a minor third, and so on, creating the Pythagorean Scale, which is so pleasing to the ear.

By counting heavenly bodies, measuring them, plotting their movements, and gauging their trajectories, you came to the conclusion that there was some pretty "high" music going on Out There.

You imagined the Sun, the Moon, and the planets to be attached to wheels or spheres—and when these wheels or spheres swiftly revolved to transport the heavenly bodies on their appointed rounds of the Earth, they emitted a musical "whoosh" or tone. The orbits were like strings on a lyre, their respective pitches determined by their respective lengths.

You said that we could actually hear this Cosmic Har-

mony produced by the Whirling of the Spheres. But, you said,
we get so accustomed to hearing it that we don't recognize it
anymore. . . .

Pythagoras's cosmology was scientific in that it tried to account for how things were and to accurately predict how they would be. Although it was inspired by the metaphysical idea of Cosmic Harmony, Pythagoras's cosmology took a giant leap in the direction of modern science-based astronomy when he suggested that the Earth was suspended in air, unsupported by anything.

Most astoundingly, Pythagoras described a World that was spherical! This is a stunning example of how cosmology evolved in fits and starts, becoming more scientifically accurate in one era and less so in a subsequent era: Pythagoras's theory that the World was a sphere held sway for only a short time before going into intellectual and cultural hibernation for centuries.

But what did the idea of a World that was round and suspended in space mean psychologically and spiritually for Pythagoras's followers? What was it about their cultural attitudes that allowed them to make that leap away from a flat disk of a World that was securely supported by *some-thing?*

For starters, like their teacher, most of Pythagoras's followers were islanders from Samos, in the Ionian Sea, so the idea of being suspended in a foreign medium might have been less unnerving for them. But what were they to make of this idea that the World was a sphere? Records do not show how Pythagoras accounted for the fact that people did not fly off this spherical Earth into the Void—there was no sign of the concept of gravity anywhere. At least some Pythagoreans must have worried about this; before Newtonian gravity was discovered, it must have been pretty hard to picture the Earth as a ball without envisioning people slipping off it.

But even if Pythagoras's view of a spherical World generated insecurities and anxieties, these were more than compensated for by his notion of Harmony. Every human being had the potential to be In Tune with everything Out There, to be a part of this Cosmic Harmony. You can tolerate some pretty scary cosmological setups if you are secure in the fact that you have an important Harmonizing Part in the Universal Song. Most important, even for a revolutionary thinker like Pythagoras, the World was still the Center of It All. And that is a very comforting thought indeed.

Earth Ego Center

There was another Greek philosopher/cosmologist who was way ahead of his time. His name was Aristarchus, he lived in the 3rd Century B.C., and like Pythagoras, his spiritual

Sistema Solare et Planetarium
OSSERVATORIO ASTRONOMICO, BRERA

grandfather, he hailed from that intellectually fertile island of Samos. Aristarchus's celestial measurements and calculations led him to a truly groundbreaking yet psychologically distressing idea: The World was *not* the Center of It All— *the Sun was!*

It is interesting how Aristarchus came to this conclusion: By comparing the sizes of the Moon and the Sun, he figured that the Sun was many times larger than the Earth; and it seemed highly unlikely that the larger body would orbit the

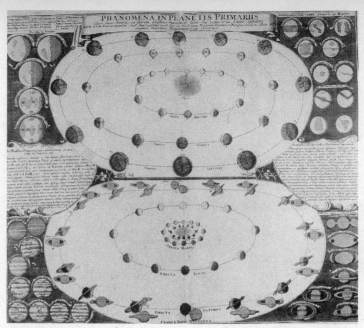

Planetis Primariis
OSSERVATORIO ASTRONOMICO, BRERA

smaller. His theory was probably based more on an intuitive sense of the relationship between size and importance than on any anticipation of Newtonian gravitational pull.

The great Greek mathematician Archimedes, a contemporary of Aristarchus, could not accept Aristarchus's heliocentrism. In what seems to us today to be circular reasoning, he argued that if the Earth was revolving around the Sun, we would have to be revolving around the stellar sphere Up There as well and "the Earth could not revolve around a sphere of which it was at the center."

Archimedes's error is understandable to anyone who re-members how shocking it was as a child to learn that the Sun doesn't actually "come up"—rather, our daily spinning brings us face-to-face with the Sun each morning. He was simply trusting his eyes to tell him the truth as any "sen-sible" person would do.

It was not just the "common sense" of naive observa-tion that Aristarchus's heliocentric theory was up against. Heliocentrism had to contend with the biggest "centrism" of them all: *ego*-centrism.

Today we live in a world where we know we are merely one of several billion people, so it might not be easy for us to get the feel of what it must have been like to live in a comprehensible world with a countable population. We might have been more subject to the vagaries of nature some twenty-odd centuries ago, but our membership in human-kind was specific and secure. We did not have to accom-modate the notion of anonymity that is thrust upon us in today's superpopulated world.

In that time and place, the World was the One Place. Most of What There Is was right here. And most of Who There Is was right here, too, ourselves accountably among them. Imagine how hard it would be to believe that this place where we live is *not* central to Everything Out There; that, in fact, where we live is just one of many such places—and not even necessarily the most important of them.

You say the Sun is the center? What about me? Until you came along with your theory, everything revolved around me and my community. The Universe was my safe and secure cave.

But now I feel like I am being swallowed up in Nothingness . . . disappearing in all this Out-Thereness. How can my life have meaning if I am suddenly an infinitesimally small speck in an Infinite Universe? How can it have significance if my geometric placement in the Universe is so arbitrary and pointless?

And tell me this: If I shout into the Void, will anyone hear me?

Unsurprisingly, Aristarchus was charged with impiety for daring to propose that the Earth was not the center of the Universe. Not long after Aristarchus's death, the very idea of heliocentrism sank into oblivion for centuries.

For the Love of Symmetry

A scant fourteen hundred years ago, astronomy and astrology were one and the same, a mix of objective fact and mythological fancy. For old-time Greek intellectuals, it did not feel inconsistent to believe both that the movement of heavenly bodies was worthy of careful objective study and that these heavenly bodies had a profound influence on our personal destinies. The former belief led to a science that was increasingly useful for quantifying time, planting crops, and navigating ships; the latter belief led to a pseudoscience that people thought was useful for figuring out what to do with their lives.

The two disciplines co-existed in this way right up until the late 6th Century A.D., when Isidorus, the bishop of Seville, drew a line in the sand separating astronomy from astrology. The bishop, of course, was less interested in protecting the sanctity of science than in putting down the fatalism of astrology—it is hard to inspire a congregation of sinners to take responsibility for their lives if they think the courses of their lives are prewritten in the stars. For a few centuries, astronomy and astrology parted ways, with only Ptolemy's astrological constellations of the Zodiac remaining a part of astronomy—a remnant of astrology that is still in astronomy to this day.

Here is a bit of history of science that I find particularly interesting: It was astrology that brought astronomy back to life after its long eclipse in the Dark Ages. In the Arab world of the early 9th Century A.D., people renewed their interest in prophecy and fortune-telling, so the casting of horoscopes made a comeback. But in order to cast a decent horoscope,

Pl. 7

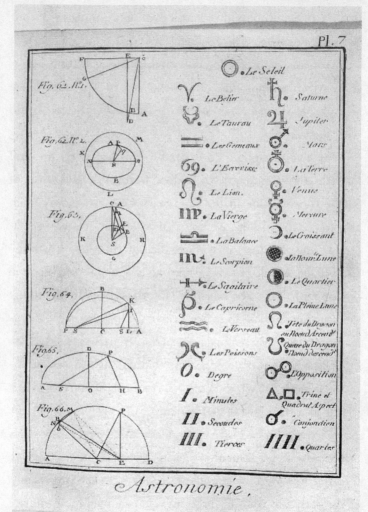

Astronomie.

Astronomie / Zodiac

OSSERVATORIO ASTRONOMICO, BRERA

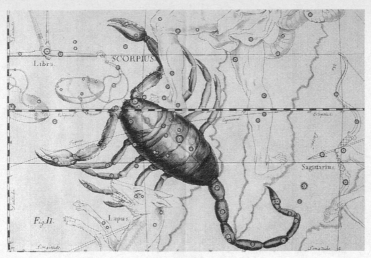

Scorpio
OSSERVATORIO ASTRONOMICO, BRERA

one needed to know a thing or two about what is going on Out There, so people like the Caliph of Baghdad built astronomical observatories to gather this information. Those old ego- and geocentric drives for a human relevance to the stars were ultimately responsible for funding the scientists.

As a scientist, I do not believe in a cause-and-effect relationship between the alignment of the planets and a person's destiny—there is simply no objective evidence of any kind that such a connection exists. However, this does not keep me from believing that there are all kinds of incredibly valuable lessons and inspirations for us to be found Out There. It would be a mistake to confuse the cause-and-effect of astrology with the metaphoric power of astronomical

Gemini

OSSERVATORIO ASTRONOMICO, BRERA

knowledge. The metaphors I find lurking everywhere in the Cosmos come to me with incredible intensity—an intensity born of the awe I feel whenever I gaze into the heavens. I am still listening for the Music of the Spheres.

One Last Cosmological Metaphor

Let me offer one final cosmological metaphor, one that came out of a collaboration with my good friend the late Timothy Leary. Tim had a genius for seeing intimate connections between seemingly irreconcilable parts of life. While often controversial, Dr. Leary was also often mis-

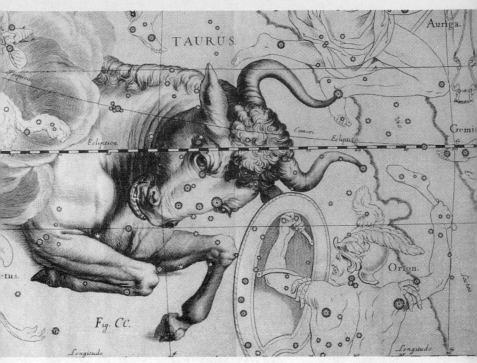

Taurus
OSSERVATORIO ASTRONOMICO, BRERA

understood. He had a truly extraordinary mind paired with an intense curiosity about the universe around him.

On one particular evening, early in our friendship, we were chatting in the library of Tim's eclectically decorated Beverly Hills home.

"Tell me, Fiorella, how many galaxies are there out there?" he suddenly asked me.

"The current estimate is around one hundred billion,"

Tim and Me
SEAN MCCALL

I replied. "And judging by the number of stars in our own Milky Way, each galaxy probably contains billions of stars."

Tim beamed, then became thoughtful.

"And what is the chemical composition of these things out there?" he asked.

"Well, stars like our Sun are made mostly of hydrogen and helium," I said. "Up to now, astrophysicists have been able to identify about seventy kinds of interstellar molecules throughout the Universe. But we are still looking, still counting."

"All molecules like those on Planet Earth?" Leary asked.

"Yes," I replied. "The very same. Chemistry has a universal signature—the same Out There as it has Down Here."

Leary burst into a magnificent grin.

"Absolutely perfect!" he said. "I love symmetry, don't you?"

"Symmetry?"

"Yes," Leary went on ex_itedly. "One hundred billion is the estimate of the _umber of neurons in one human _rain. _ne sam_ a_ _ne number of galaxies in the Universe! Now, how's that for symmetry?"

"Pretty good," I replied, smiling back.

"And both constructed out of the same molecular material here, there, everywhere," Leary went on. "The atoms of the stars whirl together in the same way that our bodies' atoms do. Maybe the human brain is a Universe Within. And like the galaxies, each neuron in our brain contributes to a tangled web of electric meanings.''

I laughed. It was another perspective on the DNA of astronomy.

''I suppose I've gone too far,'' Leary said, leaning toward me. ''I have a tendency to do that.''

''Not at all,'' I replied. ''I adore analogies between astronomy and human life.''

It was then that I told him about my work in Acoustic Astronomy, transforming radio waves from galaxies into sound. I ran through my ideas on the advantages of hearing heavenly bodies as compared with visualizing and graphing them, all the while watching his face become more and more animated.

''Exactly!'' Tim cried. ''Our brain is like an antenna. We can tune it in or tune it out. We can listen for the harmonies or we can hear only the chaos. It is up to us, isn't it?''

I think so.

Orbital Mind

We have considered the Universe from the perspective of the Earth as the center of it all. And we have considered it from the perspective of the Sun as the center, with us rotating around it. But now I want to offer a final perspective, what I call the Orbital Mind. It is the perspective of looking down from above and seeing our blue planet spinning under our feet.

Today, humankind is no longer Earthbound. We are the children of the Space Age, the first generation to escape gravity and spin with the planets and stars. We have walked on the Moon, dug into Martian soil. We have discovered active volcanoes and barren ice fields on the moons of Jupiter. We have visited the shimmering rings of Saturn. We have taken pictures of the Universe from space itself.

Space technology has given us an entirely new image of the World, and with it a new possibility for envisioning our lives. In a way, it has given each one of us wings like those that Daedalus, the master technician of ancient Greece, gave to his son, Icarus, so that he might escape his Cretan labyrinth. With this perspective, we can escape not only gravity but even the confines of the Here-and-Now. And we do not even need to be an astronaut to do this. Whenever the World is "too much with us," we can blast off for a journey of the Orbital Mind, as I so often do. I remember the first time I took this voyage. . . .

My mind has gone numb, overloaded with formulas and functions. I am into my third day—and night—in my bedroom

Earth

NASA

Astronaut Musgrave Floating in Space

NASA

in Milan, studying for my final examination in the mathematical methods of physics. If I have to analyze one more differential equation, I think my brain will implode and not a single ray of intelligence will be able to escape. . . .

The way to release myself is simple. I free myself from my earthly tether and imagine myself beginning to rise. Yes, it's working! I glance back over my shoulder—there's the top of my apartment building, two of my neighbors sunbathing. I wave. But before they can wave back, all of Milan stretches out below me—people in the streets, by the fountains, sitting in the cafés. . . .

Farther up I go. And now spreading out beneath me is the entire Lombardia region of Italy, now the Alps, too . . . now Switzerland and France. Higher I cruise, and all of Europe lies below me. Now the Atlantic . . .

And finally I am in orbit—I am the Orbital Mind, spinning around Planet Earth. Round and round I go, feeling liberated and at peace. . . .

My elliptical orbit soars deep into the darkness of space, then swings back close to my point of departure, cruising past the country hillside outside of Milan. Round I go again, sailing off into the eternal night. . . .

But this time as I glide near that Italian hillside, I behold a figure sitting in the grass, a child with her arms tightly encircling her knees as she gazes upward.

There is a look of beseeching wonder in this child's eyes.

HEAVENLY KNOWLEDGE

She looks incredibly solitary and lonely down there. . . . But she also seems miraculously at peace with herself and with everything she sees in the gaping Universe above her.

As I sail closer to this child, I glimpse a galaxy of possibilities in her wondering eyes, a constellation of heartfelt dreams. And now I hear her sweet, pure young voice calling, wailing, singing. . . .

I know this song.

I am gliding back out into the darkness again. But the song stays with me, strangely growing louder as I float farther and farther away from the child who is singing it on the Italian hillside. The song reverberates from every heavenly body I pass, echoes from every spinning sphere.

Yes, I know this song. It is the Cosmic Symphony.

And I know that child. She is me.

CODA

One Brain

by Dr. Fiorella Terenzi and Dr. Timothy Leary

The universal sounds of chemistry

Cosmic tones of physics

400 billion stars in our Milky Way Galaxy

100 billion galaxies in our Universe

Listen to the sound of stars

Open eardrums

Dilate eyeballs

Turn receivers to star-sounds

Atoms from stars whirl together

To create our bodies

15 billion years of star life—Earth life

70 kinds of interstellar molecules

The human brain

Universe within

100 billion neurons

Each neuron a tangled web of electric meanings

Limitless galaxies of meanings

Brain power. Star light.

Illumination. Enlightenment

Atoms from starlight

Random clouds of star dust

Proto planetary elements

Biogenic elements of stars like you and me

Tune brain to star-sounds

Tune brain to pulsating rhythm of star light

Tune brain to star brain

Like people stars evolve

Supernova explosions of emotion

Planetary Nebula

Energy from light-years away

Listen

Let your brain resonate

Resonate to star song

Your brain is galaxy within

Your brain is star field

Stellar life cycle

Cosmic background

Radiation, waves from our Universe

Illuminate me, star light

Enlighten me, sky glow

Fill my skull with star light

We are one

We are one, One One One BRAIN

DR. FIORELLA TERENZI

192

ACKNOWLEDGMENTS

I wish to thank Daniel Klein, for having captured my voice and vision; David Reisner, for being the friend and visionary he is; the Voyager Company for the office space and the vibrant energy; and Denisc for her mirror. My agents at William Morris Agency, especially Jonathan Trumper and Mel Berger, for keeping me in tune with the big picture, and Howard Morhaim for having made the cosmic connection with Daniel. My editor, Jennifer Hershey, for the total freedom to reach out and within. Island Records for having given me "the license to radiate." All of my professors—without their teaching I would not be here. My grandmother, mother, sister, and father—one day you will sing my songs.

I wish to thank the following astronomical facilities for their beautiful and inspiring images:
  NASA
  National Optical Astronomy Observatories
  Infrared Processing and Analysis Center, NASA
  Jet Propulsion Laboratory, NASA
  Osservatorio Astronomico, Brera, Milan

Center for Extreme Ultraviolet Astrophysics, University of California, Berkeley

Space Telescope Science Institute, Hubble Space Telescope

And my scientific consultants and technical reviewers:

Dr. Robert L. Hurt, National Research Council Fellow, IPAC/Jet Propulsion Laboratory

Dr. Laurance R. Doyle, SETI Institute, NASA Ames Research Center

Lisa M. Will, Department of Physics and Astronomy, Arizona State University

Daryl G. Parker, graduate student in astronomy and practicing law with the firm of Mahoney, Coppenrath and Jaffe

Dr. E. C. Krupp, director of the Griffith Observatory, for corrections on Celestial Architecture

Galactically Yours,
Dr. Fiorella Terenzi
e-mail: fiorella@fiorella.com

ABOUT THE AUTHOR

Dr. Fiorella Terenzi has a doctorate in physics, with specialization in astrophysics, from the University of Milan. In research at the Computer Audio Research Laboratory, University of California San Diego, she developed techniques to convert radio waves from galaxies into sound—released on her Island Records CD *Music from the Galaxies*.

Her CD-ROM *Invisible Universe* (Voyager) combined astronomy and music to present the universe beyond sight and won the Significant Achievement Award for "Most Creative Application of Multimedia in Higher and Adult Education."

Her songs are featured on the Billboard Top 20 Music Video, "The Gate to the Mind's Eye," and on the "Beyond Life" CD tribute to Dr. Timothy Leary.

She is the first astrophysicist/recording artist member of both the National Academy of Recording Arts and Sciences and the American Astronomical Society. She has studied opera and composition and taught high school/college math and physics.

In lectures—including UCSD, Stanford, MIT and Griffith Observatory—in live performances and on television, in the U.S., Europe, and Japan, Dr. Terenzi has combined science and art to awaken people to the wonders of the universe around them.

She lives in New York and Los Angeles.